Timed Readings Plus
in Mathematics

BOOK 4

15 Two-Part Lessons with Questions for
Building Reading Fluency and Comprehension

New York, New York   Columbus, Ohio   Chicago, Illinois   Peoria, Illinois   Woodland Hills, California

JAMESTOWN EDUCATION

The McGraw·Hill Companies

ISBN: 0-07-872662-X

Copyright © 2006 The McGraw-Hill Companies, Inc. All rights reserved. Except as permitted under the United States Copyright Act, no part of this publication may be reproduced or distributed in any form or by any means, or stored in a database or retrieval system, without prior written permission of the publisher.

Send all queries to:
Glencoe/McGraw-Hill
8787 Orion Place
Columbus, OH 43240-4027

2 3 4 5 6 7 8 9 10   021   10 09 08 07 06 05

CONTENTS

To the Student

    Reading Faster and Better   2

    Mastering Reading Comprehension   3

    Working Through a Lesson   7

    Plotting Your Progress   8

To the Teacher

    About the Series   9

    Timed Reading and Comprehension   10

    Speed Versus Comprehension   10

    Getting Started   10

    Timing the Reading   11

    Teaching a Lesson   11

    Monitoring Progress   12

    Diagnosis and Evaluation   12

Lessons   13–72

Answer Key   74–75

Graphs   76–78

To the Student

You probably talk at an average rate of about 150 words a minute. If you are a reader of average ability, you read at a rate of about 250 words a minute. So your reading speed is nearly twice as fast as your speaking or listening speed. This example shows that reading is one of the fastest ways to get information.

The purpose of this book is to help you increase your reading rate and understand what you read. The 15 lessons in this book will also give you practice in reading mathematics-related articles and in preparing for tests in which you must read and understand nonfiction passages within a certain time limit.

Reading Faster and Better

Following are some strategies that you can use to read the articles in each lesson.

Previewing

Previewing before you read is a very important step. This helps you to get an idea of what a selection is about and to recall any previous knowledge you have about the subject. Here are the steps to follow when previewing.

Read the title. Titles are designed not only to announce the subject but also to make the reader think. Ask yourself questions such as What can I learn from the title? What thoughts does it bring to mind? What do I already know about this subject?

Read the first sentence. If it is short, read the first two sentences. The opening sentence is the writer's opportunity to get your attention. Some writers announce what they hope to tell you in the selection. Some writers state their purpose for writing; others just try to get your attention.

Read the last sentence. If it is short, read the final two sentences. The closing sentence is the writer's last chance to get ideas across to you. Some writers repeat the main idea once more. Some writers draw a conclusion—this is what they have been leading up to. Other writers summarize their thoughts; they tie all the facts together.

Skim the entire selection. Glance through the selection quickly to see what other information you can pick up. Look for anything that will help you read fluently and with understanding. Are there names, dates, or numbers? If so, you may have to read more slowly.

Reading for Meaning

Here are some ways to make sure you are making sense of what you read.

Build your concentration. You cannot understand what you read if you are not concentrating. When you discover that your thoughts are straying, correct the situation right away. Avoid distractions and distracting situations. Keep in mind the information you learned from previewing. This will help focus your attention on the selection.

Read in thought groups. Try to see meaningful combinations of words—phrases, clauses, or sentences. If you look at only one word at a time (called word-by-word reading), both your comprehension and your reading speed suffer.

Ask yourself questions. To sustain the pace you have set for yourself and to maintain a high level of concentration and comprehension, ask yourself questions such as What does this mean? or How can I use this information? as you read.

Finding the Main Ideas

The paragraph is the basic unit of meaning. If you can quickly discover and understand the main idea of each paragraph, you will build your comprehension of the selection.

Find the topic sentence. The topic sentence, which contains the main idea, often is the first sentence of a paragraph. It is followed by sentences that support, develop, or explain the main idea. Sometimes a topic sentence comes at the end of a paragraph. When it does, the supporting details come first, building the base for the topic sentence. Some paragraphs do not have a topic sentence; all of the sentences combine to create a meaningful idea.

Understand paragraph structure. Every well-written paragraph has a purpose. The purpose may be to inform, define, explain, or illustrate. The purpose should always relate to the main idea and expand on it. As you read each paragraph, see how the body of the paragraph tells you more about the main idea.

Relate ideas as you read. As you read the selection, notice how the writer puts together ideas. As you discover the relationship between the ideas, the main ideas come through quickly and clearly.

Mastering Reading Comprehension

Reading fast is not useful if you don't remember or understand what you read. The two exercises in Part A provide a check on how well you have understood the article.

Recalling Facts

These multiple-choice questions provide a quick check to see how well you recall important information from the article. As you learn to apply the reading strategies described earlier, you should be able to answer these questions more successfully.

Understanding Ideas

These questions require you to think about the main ideas in the article. Some main ideas are stated in the article; others are not. To answer some of the questions, you need to draw conclusions about what you read.

The five exercises in Part B require multiple answers. These exercises provide practice in applying comprehension and critical thinking skills that you can use in all your reading.

Recognizing Words in Context

Always check to see whether the words around an unfamiliar word—its context—can give you a clue to the word's meaning. A word generally appears in a context related to its meaning.

Suppose, for example, that you are unsure of the meaning of the word *expired* in the following passage:

> Vera wanted to check out a book, but her library card had expired. She had to borrow my card, because she didn't have time to renew hers.

You could begin to figure out the meaning of *expired* by asking yourself a question such as, What could have happened to Vera's library card that would make her need to borrow someone else's card? You might realize that if Vera had to renew her card, its usefulness must have come to an end or run out. This would lead you to conclude that the word *expired* must mean "to come to an end" or "to run out." You would be right. The context suggested the meaning.

Context can also affect the meaning of a word you already know. The word *key*, for instance, has many meanings. There are musical keys, door keys, and keys to solving a mystery. The context in which the word *key* occurs will tell you which meaning is correct.

Sometimes a word is explained by the words that immediately follow it. The subject of a sentence and your knowledge about that subject might also help you determine the meaning of an unknown word. Try to decide the meaning of the word *revive* in the following sentence:

> Sunshine and water will revive those drooping plants.

The compound subject is *sunshine* and *water*. You know that plants need light and water to survive and that drooping plants are not healthy. You can figure out that *revive* means "to bring back to health."

Distinguishing Fact from Opinion

Every day you are called upon to sort out fact and opinion. Because much of what you read and hear contains both facts and opinions, you need to be able to tell the two apart.

Facts are statements that can be proved. The proof must be objective and verifiable. You must be able to check for yourself to confirm a fact.

Look at the following facts. Notice that they can be checked for accuracy and confirmed. Suggested sources for verification appear in parentheses.

- Abraham Lincoln was the 16th president of the United States. (Consult biographies, social studies books, encyclopedias, and similar sources.)

- Earth revolves around the Sun. (Research in encyclopedias or astronomy books; ask knowledgeable people.)
- Dogs walk on four legs. (See for yourself.)

Opinions are statements that cannot be proved. There is no objective evidence you can consult to check the truthfulness of an opinion. Unlike facts, opinions express personal beliefs or judgments. Opinions reveal how someone feels about a subject, not the facts about that subject. You might agree or disagree with someone's opinion, but you cannot prove it right or wrong.

Look at the following opinions. The reasons these statements are classified as opinions appear in parentheses.

- Abraham Lincoln was born to be a president. (You cannot prove this by referring to birth records. There is no evidence to support this belief.)
- Earth is the only planet in our solar system where intelligent life exists. (There is no proof of this. It may be proved true some day, but for now it is just an educated guess—not a fact.)
- The dog is a human's best friend. (This is not a fact; your best friend might not be a dog.)

As you read, be aware that facts and opinions are often mixed together. Both are useful to you as a reader. But to evaluate what you read and to read intelligently, you need to know the difference between the two.

Keeping Events in Order

Sequence, or chronological order, is the order of events in a story or an article or the order of steps in a process. Paying attention to the sequence of events or steps will help you follow what is happening, predict what might happen next, and make sense of a passage.

To make the sequence as clear as possible, writers often use signal words to help the reader get a more exact idea of when things happen. Following is a list of frequently used signal words and phrases:

until	first
next	then
before	after
finally	later
when	while
during	now
at the end	by the time
as soon as	in the beginning

Signal words and phrases are also useful when a writer chooses to relate details or events out of sequence. You need to pay careful attention to determine the correct chronological order.

Making Correct Inferences

Much of what you read *suggests* more than it *says*. Writers often do not state ideas directly in a text. They can't. Think of the time and space it would take to state every idea. And think of how boring that would be! Instead, writers leave it to you, the reader, to fill in the information they leave out—to make inferences. You do this by combining clues in the story or article with knowledge from your own experience.

You make many inferences every day. Suppose, for example, that you are visiting a friend's house for the first time. You see a bag of kitty litter. You infer (make an inference) that the family has a cat. Another day you overhear a conversation. You catch the names of two actors and the words *scene, dialogue,* and *directing*. You infer that the people are discussing a movie or play.

In these situations and others like them, you infer unstated information from what you observe or read. Readers must make inferences in order to understand text.

Be careful about the inferences you make. One set of facts may suggest several inferences. Some of these inferences could be faulty. A correct inference must be supported by evidence.

Remember that bag of kitty litter that caused you to infer that your friend has a cat? That could be a faulty inference. Perhaps your friend's family uses the kitty litter on their icy sidewalks to create traction. To be sure your inference is correct, you need more evidence.

Understanding Main Ideas

The main idea is the most important idea in a paragraph or passage—the idea that provides purpose and direction. The rest of the selection explains, develops, or supports the main idea. Without a main idea, there would be only a collection of unconnected thoughts.

In the following paragraph, the main idea is printed in italics. As you read, observe how the other sentences develop or explain the main idea.

Typhoon Chris hit with full fury today on the central coast of Japan. Heavy rain from the storm flooded the area. High waves carried many homes into the sea. People now fear that the heavy rains will cause mudslides in the central part of the country. The number of people killed by the storm may climb past the 200 mark by Saturday.

In this paragraph, the main idea statement appears first. It is followed by sentences that explain, support, or give details. Sometimes the main idea appears at the end of a paragraph. Writers often put the main idea at the end of a paragraph when their purpose is to persuade or convince. Readers may be more open to a new idea if the reasons for it are presented first.

As you read the following paragraph, think about the overall impact of the supporting ideas. Their purpose is to persuade the reader that the main idea in the last sentence should be accepted.

Last week there was a head-on collision at Huntington and Canton streets. Just a month ago a pedestrian was struck there. Fortunately, she was only slightly injured. In the past year, there have been more accidents there than at any other corner in the city. In fact, nearly 10 percent of all accidents in the city occur at the corner. This intersection is very dangerous, and a traffic signal should be installed there before a life is lost.

The details in the paragraph progress from least important to most important. They achieve their full effect in the main idea statement at the end.

In many cases, the main idea is not expressed in a single sentence. The reader is called upon to interpret all of the ideas expressed in the paragraph and to decide upon a main idea. Read the following paragraph.

> The American author Jack London was once a pupil at the Cole Grammar School in Oakland, California. Each morning the class sang a song. When the teacher noticed that Jack wouldn't sing, she sent him to the principal. He returned to class with a note. The note said that Jack could be excused from singing with the class if he would write an essay every morning.

In this paragraph, the reader has to interpret the individual ideas and to decide on a main idea. This main idea seems reasonable: Jack London's career as a writer began with a punishment in grammar school.

Understanding the concept of the main idea and knowing how to find it is important. Transferring that understanding to your reading and study is also important.

Working Through a Lesson

Part A

1. **Preview the article.** Locate the timed selection in Part A of the lesson that you are going to read. Wait for your teacher's signal to preview. You will have 20 seconds for previewing. Follow the previewing steps described on page 2.

2. **Read the article.** When your teacher gives you the signal, begin reading. Read carefully so that you will be able to answer questions about what you have read. When you finish reading, look at the board and note your reading time. Write this time at the bottom of the page on the line labeled Reading Time.

3. **Complete the exercises.** Answer the 10 questions that follow the article. There are 5 fact questions and 5 idea questions. Choose the best answer to each question and put an X in that box.

4. **Correct your work.** Use the Answer Key at the back of the book to check your answers. Circle any wrong answer and put an X in the box you should have marked. Record the number of correct answers on the appropriate line at the end of the lesson.

Part B

1. **Preview and read the passage.** Use the same techniques you

used to read Part A. Think about what you are reading.

2. **Complete the exercises.** Instructions are given for answering each category of question. There are 15 responses for you to record.

3. **Correct your work.** Use the Answer Key at the back of the book. Circle any wrong answer and write the correct letter or number next to it. Record the number of correct answers on the appropriate line at the end of the lesson.

Plotting Your Progress

1. **Find your reading rate.** Turn to the Reading Rate graph on page 76. Put an X at the point where the vertical line that represents the lesson intersects your reading time, shown along the left-hand side. The right-hand side of the graph will reveal your words-per-minute reading speed.

2. **Find your comprehension score.** Add your scores for Part A and Part B to determine your total number of correct answers. Turn to the Comprehension Score graph on page 77. Put an X at the point where the vertical line that represents your lesson intersects your total correct answers, shown along the left-hand side. The right-hand side of the graph will show the percentage of questions you answered correctly.

3. **Complete the Comprehension Skills Profile.** Turn to page 78. Record your incorrect answers for the Part B exercises. The five Part B skills are listed along the bottom. There are five columns of boxes, one column for each question. For every incorrect answer, put an X in a box for that skill.

To get the most benefit from these lessons, you need to take charge of your own progress in improving your reading speed and comprehension. Studying these graphs will help you to see whether your reading rate is increasing and to determine what skills you need to work on. Your teacher will also review the graphs to check your progress.

TO THE TEACHER

About the Series

Timed Readings Plus in Mathematics includes five books at reading levels 4–8, with one book at each level. Book One contains material at a fourth-grade reading level; Book Two at a fifth-grade level, and so on. The readability level is determined by the New Dale-Chall Readability Formula and is not to be confused with grade or age level of the student. The books are designed for use with students at middle school level and above.

The purposes of the series are as follows:

- to provide systematic, structured reading practice that helps students improve their reading rate and comprehension skills

- to give students practice in reading and understanding informational articles in the content area of mathematics

- to give students experience in reading various text types—informational, expository, narrative, and prescriptive

- to prepare students for taking standardized tests that include timed reading passages in various content areas

- to provide materials with a wide range of reading levels so that students can continue to practice and improve their reading rate and comprehension skills

Because the books are designed for use with students at designated reading levels rather than in a particular grade, the mathematics topics in this series are not correlated to any grade-level curriculum. Most standardized tests require students to read and comprehend mathematics passages. This series provides an opportunity for students to become familiar with the particular requirements of reading mathematics. For example, the vocabulary in a mathematics article is important. Students need to know certain words in order to understand the concepts and the information.

Each book in the series contains 15 two-part lessons. Part A focuses on improving reading rate. This section of the lesson consists of a 400-word timed informational article on a mathematics topic followed by two multiple-choice exercises. Recalling Facts includes five fact questions; Understanding Ideas includes five critical thinking questions.

Part B concentrates on building mastery in critical areas of comprehension. This section consists of a nontimed passage—the "plus" passage—followed by five exercises that address five major comprehension skills. The passage varies in length; its subject matter relates to the content of the timed selection.

Timed Reading and Comprehension

Timed reading is the best-known method of improving reading speed. There is no point in someone's reading at an accelerated speed if the person does not understand what she or he is reading. Nothing is more important than comprehension in reading. The main purpose of reading is to gain knowledge and insight, to understand the information that the writer and the text are communicating.

Few students will be able to read a passage once and answer all of the questions correctly. A score of 70 or 80 percent correct is normal. If the student gets 90 or 100 percent correct, he or she is either reading too slowly or the material is at too low a reading level. A comprehension or critical thinking score of less than 70 percent indicates a need for improvement.

One method of improving comprehension and critical thinking skills is for the student to go back and study each incorrect answer. First, the student should reread the question carefully. It is surprising how many students get the wrong answer simply because they have not read the question carefully. Then the student should look back in the passage to find the place where the question is answered, reread that part of the passage, and think about how to arrive at the correct answer. It is important to be able to recognize a correct answer when it is embedded in the text. Teacher guidance or class discussion will help the student find an answer.

Speed Versus Comprehension

It is not unusual for comprehension scores to decline as reading rate increases during the early weeks of timed readings. If this happens, students should attempt to level off their speed—but not lower it—and concentrate more on comprehension. Usually, if students maintain the higher speed and concentrate on comprehension, scores will gradually improve and within a week or two be back up to normal levels of 70 to 80 percent.

It is important to achieve a proper balance between speed and comprehension. An inefficient reader typically reads everything at one speed, usually slowly. Some poor readers, however, read rapidly but without satisfactory comprehension. The practice that this series provides enables students to increase their reading speed while maintaining normal levels of comprehension.

Getting Started

As a rule, the passages in a book designed to improve reading speed should be relatively easy. The student should not have much difficulty with the vocabulary or the subject matter. Don't worry about the passages being too easy; students should see how quickly and efficiently they can read a passage.

Begin by assigning students to a level. A student should start with a book that is one level below his or her current reading level. If a student's reading level is not known, a suitable starting point would be one or two levels below the student's present grade in school.

Introduce students to the contents and format of the book they are using. Examine the book to see how it is organized. Talk about the parts of each lesson. Discuss the purpose of timed reading and the use of the progress graphs at the back of the book.

Timing the Reading

One suggestion for timing the reading is to have all students begin reading the selection at the same time. After one minute, write on the board the time that has elapsed and begin updating it at 10-second intervals (1:00, 1:10, 1:20, etc.). Another option is to have individual students time themselves with a stopwatch.

Teaching a Lesson

Part A

1. Give students the signal to begin previewing the lesson. Allow 20 seconds, and then discuss special terms or vocabulary that students found.
2. Use one of the methods previously described to time students as they read the passage. (Include the 20-second preview time as part of the first minute.) Tell students to write down the last time shown on the board or the stopwatch when they finish reading. Have them record the time in the designated space after the passage.
3. Next, have students complete the exercises in Part A. Work with them to check their answers, using the Answer Key that begins on page 74. Have them circle incorrect answers, mark the correct answers, and then record the number of correct answers for Part A on the appropriate line at the end of the lesson. Correct responses to eight or more questions indicate satisfactory comprehension and recall.

Part B

1. Have students read the Part B passage and complete the exercises that follow it. Directions are provided with each exercise. Correct responses require deliberation and discrimination.
2. Work with students to check their answers. Then discuss the answers with them and have them record the number of correct answers for Part B at the end of the lesson.

Have students study the correct answers to the questions they answered incorrectly. It is important that they understand why a particular answer is correct or incorrect. Have them reread relevant parts of a passage to clarify an answer. An effective cooperative activity is to have students work in pairs to discuss their answers, explain why they chose the answers they did, and try to resolve differences.

Monitoring Progress

Have students find their total correct answers for the lesson and record their reading time and scores on the graphs on pages 76 and 77. Then have them complete the Comprehension Skills Profile on page 78. For each incorrect response to a question in Part B, students should mark an X in the box above each question type.

The legend on the Reading Rate graph automatically converts reading times to words-per-minute rates. The Comprehension Score graph automatically converts the raw scores to percentages.

These graphs provide a visual record of a student's progress. This record gives the student and you an opportunity to evaluate the student's progress and to determine the types of exercises and skills he or she needs to concentrate on.

Diagnosis and Evaluation

The following are typical reading rates.

Slow Reader—150 Words Per Minute

Average Reader—250 Words Per Minute

Fast Reader—350 Words Per Minute

A student who consistently reads at an average or above-average rate (with satisfactory comprehension) is ready to advance to the next book in the series.

A column of X's in the Comprehension Skills Profile indicates a specific comprehension weakness. Using the profile, you can assess trends in student performance and suggest remedial work if necessary.

1 A   A History of Calculators

A calculator is a small, fast, accurate tool for solving mathematical problems. The earliest "calculator" was the counting board, used in Babylonia more than 2,000 years ago. The counting board was a portable, flat surface made out of wood or stone with grooves cut into it. Beads or pebbles were moved along the grooves to add, subtract, and show place value.

The abacus is believed to have evolved from the counting board. The earliest known use of the abacus was in China around 1200. To add, subtract, divide, and multiply on an abacus, beads are moved along parallel rods. The rods are divided into upper and lower brackets. Each rod stands for a place value, and each bead represents either a value of five in the upper bracket or a value of one in the lower bracket. Some people still use the abacus.

The discovery of the logarithm in 1614 led to the invention of the slide rule in 1625. The logarithm, discovered by John Napier, made it possible to multiply and divide by addition and subtraction. The modern slide rule has two flat bars that look like rulers held together by a cursor. The cursor moves along the center of the instrument, aligning with the logarithmic scales on the upper and lower bars. By lining up the logarithms on the bars in certain ways, users can make calculations quickly and easily. Until the invention of the electronic calculator, people whose work depended on complex calculations used slide rules.

In the 20th century, the adding machine was commonly used in business and accounting to perform basic calculations. This machine printed its calculations on a paper tape. It was simple to operate and could be used by people with very little mathematical knowledge. The user entered a number on the keyboard and then pulled down a crank to print the number on the tape and add the number to a running total. Electric power later replaced manual crank power.

By the mid-1960s, the first battery-operated calculator with integrated circuits arrived on the scene. By 1972 the calculator could do complex algebra and other special functions. Also it could be programmed to use scientific notation. The solar-powered calculator appeared soon after. Pocket-sized and with a larger memory, the calculator replaced the slide rule in science and math classrooms. Modern calculators have ports that make it possible to copy data to and from computers.

Reading Time _____

Recalling Facts

1. Counting boards
   - a. are also called slide rules.
   - b. were used in Babylonia more than 2,000 years ago.
   - c. evolved from the abacus.

2. To calculate using a slide rule, the user
   - a. lines up numbers on moving bars.
   - b. moves beads along rods in upper and lower brackets.
   - c. moves a cursor, aligning it with the logarithmic scales on upper and lower bars.

3. The discovery of the logarithm
   - a. led to the invention of the slide rule.
   - b. led to the invention of the electronic calculator.
   - c. occurred after the slide rule was invented.

4. Early adding machines were used
   - a. to perform basic calculations.
   - b. to perform logarithms.
   - c. mainly by mathematicians.

5. The first battery-operated calculator with integrated circuits arrived on the scene in the
   - a. 1950s.
   - b. 1960s.
   - c. 1970s.

Understanding Ideas

6. The abacus was an improvement on the counting board because it could be
   - a. used to multiply and divide.
   - b. moved from place to place.
   - c. used to add and subtract.

7. Slide rules probably are no longer used in schools because
   - a. logarithms are no longer used.
   - b. they are less accurate than calculators.
   - c. calculators are faster and easier to use.

8. One can conclude from the passage that mathematicians did not use adding machines because they
   - a. were heavy and difficult to use.
   - b. could not perform complex calculations.
   - c. were used only in business.

9. One can conclude that integrated circuits allowed calculators to
   - a. move from manual to battery power.
   - b. use solar power.
   - c. do more mathematical functions faster.

10. Which statement best summarizes the passage?
    - a. No further advances can be made in the development of the electronic calculator.
    - b. Almost every advance in the development of the modern calculator was based on a previous discovery or advance.
    - c. Every important advance in the development of the calculator has occurred since 1972.

1 B Ada Byron, Lady Lovelace

Ada Byron Lovelace, the daughter of British poet Lord Byron, was born in 1815. When she was 17, she met Charles Babbage, a mathematics professor. She became intrigued by his plans for a new kind of calculating machine called the Analytical Engine. Ada had received tutoring in mathematics, but as a woman, she was not allowed to attend a university. Babbage encouraged her interest in mathematics. They wrote long letters to each other about mathematics, logic, and many other subjects.

   Babbage continued working on the plans for his engine. In 1841 he reported on his developments, and a summary of his plans was published in an article in French. Babbage asked Ada to translate the article. When she showed him the translation, he suggested that she add her own notes to it. In 1843 Ada, now Lady Lovelace by her marriage to the Earl of Lovelace, published the article. In it she predicted that the machine could be used to compose complex music and to produce graphics—in short, for both practical and scientific purposes. Later she suggested to Babbage how the Analytical Engine might calculate complex numbers used in algebra. This plan is now regarded as the first computer program.

1. **Recognizing Words in Context**

   Find the word *intrigued* in the passage. One definition below is closest to the meaning of that word. One definition has the opposite or nearly the opposite meaning. The remaining definition has a completely different meaning. Label the definitions C for *closest*, O for *opposite or nearly opposite*, and D for *different*.

   _____ a. saddened
   _____ b. interested
   _____ c. indifferent

2. **Distinguishing Fact from Opinion**

   Two of the statements below present *facts*, which can be proved. The other statement is an *opinion*, which expresses someone's thoughts or beliefs. Label the statements F for *fact* and O for *opinion*.

   _____ a. Babbage suggested that Ada add her own notes to the translation.
   _____ b. Ada could have built Babbage's invention herself.
   _____ c. Babbage encouraged Ada's interest in mathematics.

3. **Keeping Events in Order**

   Number the statements below 1, 2, and 3 to show the order in which the events took place.

   _____ a. Ada Byron published an article explaining the Analytical Engine.

   _____ b. Ada Byron created the first computer program.

   _____ c. Ada met Charles Babbage.

4. **Making Correct Inferences**

   Two of the statements below are correct *inferences,* or reasonable guesses. They are based on information in the passage. The other statement is an incorrect, or faulty, inference. Label the statements C for *correct* inference and F for *faulty* inference.

   _____ a. Without Babbage's help, Ada would not be known as a mathematician today.

   _____ b. Babbage asked Ada to add her own ideas to the article because he liked them.

   _____ c. The fact that Ada suggested how the Analytical Engine might calculate complex numbers means that she knew how to calculate them.

5. **Understanding Main Ideas**

   One of the statements below expresses the main idea of the passage. One statement is too general, or too broad. The other explains only part of the passage; it is too narrow. Label the statements M for *main idea,* B for *too broad,* and N for *too narrow.*

   _____ a. Ada Byron Lovelace worked with Charles Babbage on his plans for the Analytical Engine.

   _____ b. Ada Byron Lovelace and Charles Babbage were pioneers in the development of the computer.

   _____ c. Ada Byron Lovelace, without any formal education in mathematics, invented the first computer program.

Correct Answers, Part A _____

Correct Answers, Part B _____

Total Correct Answers _____

2 A   Tracking Falkland Island Penguins

Several species of penguin are found in the Falkland Islands, which are about 300 miles northeast of the southern tip of South America. In 1998 two species, the Magellanic and the rockhopper penguins, were part of a three-month study of winter migration patterns.

During the winter season, penguins migrate long distances toward the coast of South America. Ten Magellanic and five rockhopper penguins were fitted with satellite transmitters to track the penguins' migration. The satellite received signals sent by the transmitters. Computers on the ground then calculated the transmitters' latitude and longitude. The data were analyzed to compare speeds, distances, and routes traveled by the two species. Averages calculated for traveling speed were considered the minimum, because it was assumed that penguins move in a straight line between locations.

Magellanic penguins usually head northwest during their winter migration. They swim either in the coastal waters of South America or farther offshore. All of the birds but one headed for the same area, but did so using two different routes. Although the number of miles traveled by the birds varied, all but one eventually reached the same area, 1,125 miles from their home. One penguin traveled to a different site, some 625 miles from home. The greatest distance traveled by one Magellanic penguin was 1,663 miles in 75 days.

The pattern of movement for the rockhopper penguins was not as clear. These birds tend to swim in large circles until one of them sees a land mass. As a result, the migration of rockhopper penguins takes much longer. Three of the penguins traveled farther to the west than the Magellanic penguins did. The greatest distance from home reached by one of these birds was about 437 miles. The other two birds traveled north. One of them kept rather close to the islands and even returned home several times. The other bird traveled a total distance of 1,324 miles in 75 days.

It was clear from the data collected by satellite tracking that Magellanic penguins travel much farther than rockhopper penguins do. The traveling speed of each species was also different. Magellanic penguins, on average, traveled about 22 miles per day. The rockhoppers traveled an average of 12 miles per day. So each day the Magellanic penguins traveled 10 miles farther and about 83 percent faster (22 miles − 12 miles = 10 miles; 10 miles ÷ 12 miles = .83) than the rockhoppers.

Reading Time _____

Recalling Facts

1. Several breeds of penguins are found in the Falkland Islands, a group of islands
   - a. off the western part of Africa.
   - b. near the United Kingdom.
   - c. off the southern tip of South America.

2. Magellanic and rockhopper penguins, were a part of a three-month study
   - a. of the penguins' winter migration patterns.
   - b. to test a computer satellite tracking system.
   - c. to help penguins find food and breeding places.

3. The 1998 study revealed that during migration, all but one of the Magellanic penguins headed for the same area using
   - a. many routes.
   - b. two routes.
   - c. the same route.

4. The study found that the pattern of movement for the rockhopper penguins
   - a. was the same as the pattern for Magellanic penguins.
   - b. was clear and easily tracked.
   - c. was not as clear as the pattern for Magellanic penguins.

5. Magellanic penguins travel at a speed of
   - a. 44 miles per day.
   - b. 12 miles per day.
   - c. 22 miles per day.

Understanding Ideas

6. One can conclude from the passage that during winter migration,
   - a. Magellanic penguins prefer to stay closer to home.
   - b. both Magellanic and rockhopper penguins travel the same distance from home.
   - c. rockhopper penguins prefer to stay closer to home.

7. A penguin's swimming speed can be calculated by finding out
   - a. in what direction the bird traveled from home.
   - b. how long it took the bird to travel between two points.
   - c. how far from home the bird was swimming.

8. Penguins that swim in large circles before going in a certain direction
   - a. swim faster than other penguins.
   - b. will travel a shorter distance over time than other penguins.
   - c. will travel farther over time than other penguins.

9. One can conclude that Magellanic penguins, in general,
   - a. migrate in many directions.
   - b. stay close to home.
   - c. migrate as a group.

10. One can conclude that if a transmitter had stopped working for a short time,
    - a. the study would have been called off.
    - b. the averages calculated for that penguin would have been adjusted.
    - c. data from previous years would have been used to cover for that gap in time.

2 B The Population of Giant Pandas

Giant pandas, which live in the mountainous forests of western China and eastern Tibet, are endangered animals. Hunting and land development have threatened the pandas and their habitat. In the mid-1970s, only about 1,100 giant pandas were known to be living in the wild. The number remained unchanged in the next panda population survey. That survey was conducted from 1985 to 1988 by the Chinese government and the World Wildlife Fund (WWF). Now, however, the panda population has risen dramatically. A study done from 2000 to 2004 by China and the WWF showed that about 1,600 giant pandas were living in the wild. This is about a 45 percent increase since the previous survey.

   Some experts question whether the rise in the number of pandas is truly this great. They suspect that earlier counts underestimated the number of pandas. They believe that the use of the Global Positioning System (GPS) to track pandas in the 2000–2004 study gave a more accurate count. GPS is a constellation of satellites that helps a person with a receiver calculate his or her position on Earth. A GPS receiver uses the satellites' radio signals as reference points to find a position. Because earlier studies of pandas did not use GPS, the correct percent of increase in the panda population is in question.

1. **Recognizing Words in Context**

   Find the word *endangered* in the passage. One definition below is closest to the meaning of that word. One definition has the opposite or nearly the opposite meaning. The remaining definition has a completely different meaning. Label the definitions C for *closest*, O for *opposite or nearly opposite*, and D for *different*.

   _____ a. resourceful

   _____ b. scarce

   _____ c. plentiful

2. **Distinguishing Fact from Opinion**

   Two of the statements below present *facts*, which can be proved. The other statement is an *opinion*, which expresses someone's thoughts or beliefs. Label the statements F for *fact* and O for *opinion*.

   _____ a. GPS is used to find positions on Earth.

   _____ b. Conservation efforts are the best way to save the pandas.

   _____ c. A study showed that the number of pandas in the wild had increased to 1,600.

3. **Keeping Events in Order**

    Number the statements below 1, 2, and 3 to show the order in which the events took place.

    _____ a. Statistics showed that there are about 1,600 giant pandas living in the wild.

    _____ b. The number of giant pandas known to be living in the wild remained unchanged.

    _____ c. Only 1,100 giant pandas were known to be alive in the wild.

4. **Making Correct Inferences**

    Two of the statements below are correct *inferences,* or reasonable guesses. They are based on information in the passage. The other statement is an incorrect, or faulty, inference. Label the statements C for *correct* inference and F for *faulty* inference.

    _____ a. The number of giant pandas has grown since the 1980s.

    _____ b. The 2000–2004 statistics are inaccurate because GPS was used.

    _____ c. Creating wildlife preserves where giant pandas can live will help protect them.

5. **Understanding Main Ideas**

    One of the statements below expresses the main idea of the passage. One statement is too general, or too broad. The other explains only part of the passage; it is too narrow. Label the statements M for *main idea,* B for *too broad,* and N for *too narrow.*

    _____ a. Giant pandas live in western China and eastern Tibet.

    _____ b. The giant panda population is growing, but by how much is unclear.

    _____ c. The giant panda is just one of many endangered animals that live in China.

Correct Answers, Part A _____

Correct Answers, Part B _____

Total Correct Answers _____

3 A What Is Algebra?

Algebra is the branch of mathematics in which letters represent unknown variables in math equations. An equation is a mathematical sentence stating that two expressions are equal, such as $3x + y = 7$. Algebra is used in business and industry to help solve many problems.

In algebra, letters such as x and y are called variables and represent unknown numbers. When we "solve an equation," we search for a value that would balance the two sides of the equation. A simple example is the equation $x + 4 = 9$. This statement is true only when x equals 5, because $5 + 4 = 9$. Another example is the equation $14 - x = 6$. This statement is true only when x equals 8, because $14 - 8 = 6$.

What is the value for y in the equation $176 + y = 477$? It's as though you have a balance beam with a mystery box on one side. You're either adding the same weight on each side or removing the same weight from each side until you figure out exactly how much that mystery box weighs. To solve the problem, keep both sides of the equation equal. Perform the same operation on each side to isolate the variable y on one side of the equation. To isolate a variable, use the inverse—or opposite—function that the equation uses. The equation $176 + y = 477$ is an addition problem, so the inverse function is subtraction. Subtracting the same amount from each side of the equation keeps the sides equal. The new equation would be $176 + y - 176 = 477 - 176$. On the left side of the equation, only y remains. On the right side of the equation, $477 - 176 = 301$. Because both sides of the equation are equal, y must also equal 301.

Look at the equation $x \times 14 = 308$. Another way to write this equation is $14x = 308$. To find the value for x, isolate the variable x on one side of the equation. Perform the inverse operation on each side of the equation. In the equation $14x = 308$, x is isolated by dividing each side of the equation by 14. The left side of the equation shows $14x \div 14 = 1x$. Any number multiplied by 1 is itself, so $1x$ is the same as x. Now the equation reads $x = 308 \div 14$. Then divide 308 by 14, which is 22. Because both sides are always equal, $x = 22$.

Reading Time _____

Recalling Facts

1. In algebra, letters that represent unknown numbers are
   - a. variables.
   - b. isolations.
   - c. equations.

2. An equation is a kind of mathematical sentence that says two expressions are
   - a. inverse.
   - b. variable.
   - c. equal.

3. In some problems, the value of each variable must remain
   - a. an expression.
   - b. isolated.
   - c. the same.

4. To isolate a variable, we use the _____ function.
   - a. multiplication
   - b. inverse
   - c. subtraction

5. In the equation $14y = 308$, $14y$ means
   - a. $14 \div y$.
   - b. $14 \times y$.
   - c. $14 + y$.

Understanding Ideas

6. One can conclude from the information in this passage that
   - a. algebra is another way to learn addition and subtraction.
   - b. algebra is used to find a value for an unknown variable.
   - c. algebra equations can best be answered through trial and error.

7. If an equation calls for addition, the inverse function would be
   - a. subtraction.
   - b. multiplication.
   - c. division.

8. In the equation $15 + y = 22$, to isolate y one should
   - a. subtract 15 from each side of the equation.
   - b. add 15 to each side of the equation.
   - c. subtract 22 from 15.

9. In the equation $6x = 36$, x equals
   - a. 6.
   - b. 30.
   - c. 42.

10. What is the clue that serves as a reminder that both sides of the equation are equal?
    - a. the variable
    - b. the function sign
    - c. the equal sign

3 B Algebra to Go

Skye has tickets for tonight's concert. She has a soccer game and other things to do first, so she isn't sure whether she will have adequate time to get ready. Examining her watch, Skye observes that it is exactly noon. The concert begins in 8 hours, and she'll need about 4½ hours to shower, get a manicure, and eat something. A soccer game usually lasts about 1¾ hours. Skye wants to know how much free time she'll have before the concert.

    Skye decides to create a math equation to help her solve the problem. She finds a scrap of paper and a pencil in her backpack. First she writes the numbers she knows. The soccer game will take 1¾ hours, and the shower, manicure, and meal will take another 4½ hours. The variable x represents the amount of time that will remain, and 8 hours is how long she has until the concert starts. Skye writes her equation: 1¾ + 4½ + x = 8. Next she adds the two known numbers on the left side to get just one number: 1¾ + 4½ = 6¼. Then she isolates the variable x: 6¼ + x − 6¼ = 8 − 6¼. She sees that x = 1¾ hours of free time remaining before the concert.

1. **Recognizing Words in Context**

   Find the word *adequate* in the passage. One definition below is closest to the meaning of that word. One definition has the opposite or nearly the opposite meaning. The remaining definition has a completely different meaning. Label the definitions C for *closest*, O for *opposite or nearly opposite*, and D for *different*.

   _____ a. enough

   _____ b. restricted

   _____ c. too little

2. **Distinguishing Fact from Opinion**

   Two of the statements below present *facts*, which can be proved. The other statement is an *opinion*, which expresses someone's thoughts or beliefs. Label the statements F for *fact* and O for *opinion*.

   _____ a. Skye doesn't need more than two hours to get ready for the concert.

   _____ b. Skye needs about 4½ hours to finish doing other things after the soccer game.

   _____ c. Skye's soccer games usually last about 1¾ hours.

3. **Keeping Events in Order**

   Number the statements below 1, 2, and 3 to show the order in which the events take place.

   _____ a. Skye creates an algebra equation that helps her find out how much free time she will have left.

   _____ b. Skye plays soccer.

   _____ c. Skye buys tickets for the concert.

4. **Making Correct Inferences**

   Two of the statements below are correct *inferences,* or reasonable guesses. They are based on information in the passage. The other statement is an incorrect, or faulty, inference. Label the statements C for *correct* inference and F for *faulty* inference.

   _____ a. Skye realizes that she has no time left to get her manicure before the concert.

   _____ b. If Skye actually has less than 1¾ hours, it will be because her "known" numbers are wrong.

   _____ c. Finding what the variable stands for depends on the other numbers in the equation.

5. **Understanding Main Ideas**

   One of the statements below expresses the main idea of the passage. One statement is too general, or too broad. The other explains only part of the passage; it is too narrow. Label the statements M for *main idea,* B for *too broad,* and N for *too narrow.*

   _____ a. Skye finds out how much free time she has left by using algebra.

   _____ b. Skye creates a math equation to help her solve a problem.

   _____ c. Skye wants to know whether she has enough time to do everything.

   Correct Answers, Part A _____

   Correct Answers, Part B _____

   Total Correct Answers _____

4 A

Ancient Egyptian Mathematics

Ancient cultures fascinated Scottish lawyer A. Henry Rhind. On a trip to Egypt in 1858, he bought a remarkable papyrus. Papyrus is a paper made from the grasslike plant of the same name. The Rhind Papyrus is a scroll 13 inches wide and 18 feet long. It is at least 3,500 years old, and the writing on it is hieratic script, a form of Egyptian writing. The writer was a scribe named Ahmes. But Ahmes did not create the text; he copied a text written about 200 years earlier.

The Rhind Papyrus is a guide to ancient Egyptian mathematics. The scroll shows how to do many things, such as figure out the volume of a cylinder or the area of a triangle or circle. It also contains a table with the answers to many common arithmetic problems. Looking up the answers in the table often took less time than figuring out even a simple problem.

Ancient Egyptian math was awkward compared with the way we do things now. Numbers had to be written out. The number 32, for instance, was written "10 10 10 1 1." Egyptians didn't use a "plus" sign. They could add and subtract any numbers, but they could multiply and divide only by 2. Multiplication, therefore, required a complicated series of actions that included doubling, subtracting, and adding.

Ancient Egyptian math got even more difficult when working with fractions. Except for the fraction $\frac{2}{3}$, Egyptians used only unit fractions in their writing. A unit fraction must have a 1 in the numerator; $\frac{1}{2}$, $\frac{1}{3}$, and $\frac{1}{4}$ are unit fractions. The Egyptians would have written the fraction $\frac{3}{4}$, for instance, as $\frac{1}{2}$ $\frac{1}{4}$. They had rules about how to write fractions. One rule was that the same fraction could not be used more than once in a number. The fraction $\frac{9}{10}$, for instance, could not be written $\frac{1}{2}$ $\frac{1}{5}$ $\frac{1}{5}$. The correct way to write $\frac{9}{10}$ would have been $\frac{2}{3}$ $\frac{1}{5}$ $\frac{1}{30}$.

Rhind died in 1863, just five years after he acquired the papyrus. When the British Museum in London, England, received the papyrus and other valuable items that Rhind had bequeathed to the museum, some pieces of the papyrus were missing. Later, these fragments were said to have been found in a collection of the Brooklyn Museum in New York.

Reading Time ______

Recalling Facts

1. The Rhind Papyrus was written
   - a. in ink on parchment.
   - b. in hieroglyphics.
   - c. in hieratic script.

2. The Rhind Papyrus is a
   - a. guide to Egyptian mathematics.
   - b. document about the history of math.
   - c. book for teaching math.

3. Papyrus is a type of
   - a. language.
   - b. book.
   - c. paper.

4. The ancient Egyptians used only
   - a. mixed fractions.
   - b. unit fractions and the fraction $\frac{2}{3}$.
   - c. regular fractions.

5. The Rhind Papyrus was written
   - a. in 1858.
   - b. by an Egyptian mathematician.
   - c. more than 3,500 years ago.

Understanding Ideas

6. It is likely that the quality most useful in an Egyptian scribe was
   - a. imagination.
   - b. accuracy.
   - c. wisdom.

7. Which of the following would be the correct way for an ancient Egyptian to write the fraction "four-fifths"?
   - a. $\frac{4}{5}$
   - b. $\frac{1}{4}\ \frac{1}{4}\ \frac{1}{4}\ \frac{1}{20}$
   - c. $\frac{1}{2}\ \frac{1}{4}\ \frac{1}{20}$

8. An object that has been "bequeathed" is
   - a. something that has been purchased.
   - b. a gift from someone.
   - c. usually a surprise.

9. One can infer from this passage that the ancient Egyptians
   - a. did not understand fractions.
   - b. could solve many mathematical problems.
   - c. believed that only educated people could do math.

10. It is likely that the Egyptians didn't use a "plus" sign because
    - a. numbers grouped together were meant to be added.
    - b. they used only a "minus" sign.
    - c. addition was understood as a form of multiplication.

4 B Counting Like an Egyptian

Although the ancient Egyptians created different symbols for numbers, they used a base-10 counting system like we use today. In base-10, things are placed in groups of 10—ten ones are 10, ten tens are 100, ten hundreds are 1,000, and so on.

The earliest form of Egyptian writing is called hieroglyphics. Hieroglyphs are pictures and patterns that symbolize a word or an idea. In hieroglyphics, the number 1 is represented by a vertical stroke; in fact, the hieroglyphic 1 looks similar to our number 1. The numbers 2 through 9 are clusters of these strokes. The 10 resembles a little arch or an upside-down "U." The hieroglyphic 100 looks like a comma with a long tail. Three "commas" followed by four strokes, for instance, represent the number 304. There are also hieroglyphs for 1,000, 100,000, and 1,000,000.

The successor of hieroglyphics, hieratic script, uses individual symbols for each number. Numbers 1 through 9 are assigned unique symbols. So are each unit of tens, from 10 to 90, each unit of hundreds, and each unit of thousands. It is easy to spot similarities between these two scripts. The hieratic 10 looks like an upside-down "V" instead of the hieroglyphic upside-down "U." The hieratic 100 also looks like a comma with a long tail, only more so. It takes 36 hieroglyphs to write the number 9,999. But it takes only four hieratic symbols.

1. **Recognizing Words in Context**

   Find the word *successor* in the passage. One definition below is closest to the meaning of that word. One definition has the opposite or nearly the opposite meaning. The remaining definition has a completely different meaning. Label the definitions C for *closest*, O for *opposite or nearly opposite*, and D for *different*.

   _____ a. supervisor

   _____ b. replacement

   _____ c. ancestor

2. **Distinguishing Fact from Opinion**

   Two of the statements below present *facts*, which can be proved. The other statement is an *opinion*, which expresses someone's thoughts or beliefs. Label the statements F for *fact* and O for *opinion*.

   _____ a. Hieratic script was an improvement over hieroglyphics.

   _____ b. It often took many hieroglyphs to write a number.

   _____ c. Hieroglyphs are pictures and patterns that symbolize an idea.

3. **Keeping Events in Order**

   Number the answers below 1, 2, and 3 to show the order in which the events took place.

   _____ a. use of hieratic script

   _____ b. use of Arabic numerals

   _____ c. use of hieroglyphs

4. **Making Correct Inferences**

   Two of the statements below are correct *inferences,* or reasonable guesses. They are based on information in the passage. The other statement is an incorrect, or faulty, inference. Label the statements C for *correct* inference and F for *faulty* inference.

   _____ a. There are more symbols for numbers in hieratic script than in hieroglyphics.

   _____ b. Arabic numerals are based on hieratic script.

   _____ c. Hieratic script is related to hieroglyphics.

5. **Understanding Main Ideas**

   One of the statements below expresses the main idea of the passage. One statement is too general, or too broad. The other explains only part of the passage; it is too narrow. Label the statements M for *main idea,* B for *too broad,* and N for *too narrow.*

   _____ a. Ancient Egyptians developed different ways of writing numbers.

   _____ b. The number 100 looks about the same in both hieroglyphics and hieratic script.

   _____ c. Egyptians used two scripts for writing numbers in a base-10 counting system.

Correct Answers, Part A _____

Correct Answers, Part B _____

Total Correct Answers _____

5 A The History and Use of Bar Codes

In the second half of the 20th century, there were dramatic advances in information technologies. One area of advancement was in the use of mathematical codes. People used the codes to track information, to detect data errors, and to provide security.

One type of code is the bar code. A bar code makes it possible for people to identify an object and quickly find information about it in their computer systems. Today people use bar codes to track express mail, airport luggage, and library books. Those in the medical field and in the military also use bar codes.

Retailers have used one type of bar code called the Universal Product Code (UPC) since 1973. A UPC is on almost every product you buy. It identifies the product and the company that makes it. Stores use UPCs for pricing and to track the sale of goods. The UPC allows stores to create a database with information about all the goods they sell.

There are a number of types of UPCs. The most common type has 12 digits. The first six digits tell what company makes the product. The next five digits identify the product. The last digit is called the check digit. The check digit detects human error when a code is entered into a store's database. Sometimes a worker may switch numbers or key in a wrong number. The check digit not only detects the error but also corrects it.

Here is an example of how the check digit works. To determine the check digit for a UPC, look at the first 11 digits of the bar code; for example, 0 12345 43210. Step 1 is to find the sum of the even-numbered digits, 0, 2, 4, 4, 2, and 0. That sum is 12. Step 2 is to multiply this sum by 3; $12 \times 3 = 36$. Step 3 is to find the sum of the odd-numbered digits, 1, 3, 5, 3, and 1. This sum is 13. Step 4 is to add the answers from Step 2 and Step 3; $36 + 13 = 49$. Step 5 is to subtract this sum from the next-highest multiple of 10, which is 50; $50 - 49 = 1$. The check digit for this UPC is 1. If an employee makes a mistake entering the UPC numbers into the database, the check digit shows and corrects the error.

Reading Time _____

Recalling Facts

1. A bar code makes it possible for people to
   - ❏ a. identify an object and find information about it in a computer system.
   - ❏ b. perform calculations quickly.
   - ❏ c. track time for a task.

2. The Universal Product Code (UPC) is a type of bar code used by
   - ❏ a. retailers.
   - ❏ b. doctors.
   - ❏ c. librarians.

3. Stores use the UPC
   - ❏ a. for security reasons.
   - ❏ b. for pricing and tracking the sale of goods.
   - ❏ c. to track employees' pay.

4. The most common type of UPC has
   - ❏ a. 3 digits.
   - ❏ b. 5 digits.
   - ❏ c. 12 digits.

5. If an employee makes a mistake entering a UPC into a database, the check digit
   - ❏ a. does not function.
   - ❏ b. shows and corrects the error.
   - ❏ c. tracks the sale of goods.

Understanding Ideas

6. It is likely that bar codes were not used before the second half of the 20th century because
   - ❏ a. stores were not as busy.
   - ❏ b. stores did not stock as many products.
   - ❏ c. the technology was not available.

7. Bar codes would most likely be used to track
   - ❏ a. freight at a shipping company.
   - ❏ b. the sale of gasoline at a gas station.
   - ❏ c. the arrival and departure of buses at a bus station.

8. To determine the check digit for a UPC, a person must use
   - ❏ a. multiplication and division.
   - ❏ b. addition and division.
   - ❏ c. addition, subtraction, and multiplication.

9. Which of the following can one conclude was *not* a purpose of the UPC?
   - ❏ a. automated pricing
   - ❏ b. databases for store goods
   - ❏ c. increased store security

10. It is likely that one advancement made as a result of the invention of UPCs is
    - ❏ a. computerized product ordering.
    - ❏ b. computerized methods of payment.
    - ❏ c. computerized time clocks for employees.

5 B Bar Codes for Books

The ISBN, or International Standard Book Number, is a bar code that publishers use to track and identify books. It is used for almost every book in the world. The code consists of 10 digits divided into four blocks. Block 1 identifies the country, area, or language area of the book. Block 1 for an English language book is 0, whereas books published for readers in India use the number 8. Block 2 is the publisher's number. Block 3 is the item number of the book. Block 4, the last digit, is the check digit. The ISBN check digit detects errors but does not correct them.

A simple mathematical procedure determines the check digit. For example, take the first nine digits of a made-up ISBN: 0-234-56789. To find the check digit, multiply the first digit by 10, the second digit by 9, the third digit by 8, etc. Then add the products. The check digit will be the number that, when added to this sum, makes the total divisible by 11. In this case, the sum of the products is 200, so the check digit is 9 (200 + 9 = 209, which is divisible by 11).

1. **Recognizing Words in Context**

   Find the word *detects* in the passage. One definition below is closest to the meaning of that word. One definition has the opposite or nearly the opposite meaning. The remaining definition has a completely different meaning. Label the definitions C for *closest,* O for *opposite or nearly opposite,* and D for *different.*

   _____ a. finds
   _____ b. loses
   _____ c. hides

2. **Distinguishing Fact from Opinion**

   Two of the statements below present *facts,* which can be proved. The other statement is an *opinion,* which expresses someone's thoughts or beliefs. Label the statements F for *fact* and O for *opinion.*

   _____ a. ISBNs have check digits to detect numerical errors.
   _____ b. The idea of a check digit is brilliant.
   _____ c. ISBNs are used for almost every book in the world.

3. **Keeping Events in Order**

   Number the statements below 1, 2, and 3 to show the order of the blocks of numbers in an ISBN.

   _____ a. check digit

   _____ b. country, area, or language area

   _____ c. publisher and item numbers

4. **Making Correct Inferences**

   Two of the statements below are correct *inferences,* or reasonable guesses. They are based on information in the passage. The other statement is an incorrect, or faulty, inference. Label the statements C for *correct* inference and F for *faulty* inference.

   _____ a. Publishers do not use ISBNs.

   _____ b. ISBNs have gained international acceptance.

   _____ c. The inventors of ISBNs were concerned about preventing errors in the code.

5. **Understanding Main Ideas**

   One of the statements below expresses the main idea of the passage. One statement is too general, or too broad. The other explains only part of the passage; it is too narrow. Label the statements M for *main idea,* B for *too broad,* and N for *too narrow.*

   _____ a. The use of codes has grown with advances in technology.

   _____ b. ISBNs are bar codes used to identify and track books.

   _____ c. ISBNs have 10 digits.

Correct Answers, Part A _____

Correct Answers, Part B _____

Total Correct Answers _____

6 A Putting Music on Compact Discs

Since they were first sold in the 1980s, compact discs (CDs) have been a popular means of listening to recorded music. The older, long-playing records and audiotapes are easily scratched and damaged. CDs, however, given reasonable care, almost never wear out. Not only are they made from durable materials, but they are "played" by a beam of light. A needle moving through the grooves of a vinyl record can scratch and damage the record's surface, but the beam of light does not leave a mark on a CD. CD technology is also used to make video recordings, such as digital video discs (DVDs).

In the making of a CD, a microphone captures sound waves in a process called signal sampling. The amplitude, or size, of each sound wave or signal is measured many times per second. Up to 65,000 samples can be taken each second, but most CDs use 44,100 samples per second. The more samples taken, the more accurate or true the sound produced by the CD. Each sample is saved, or "digitized," as binary code. Binary code has only two symbols, or digits, a "0" and a "1." Each sample of sound, therefore, is a string of 16 "bits," or binary digits of binary code.

Most recordings are stereo; they separate sound into two channels. Each channel produces its own string of code, and both strings are cut into the CD. How many bits of code are in one second of music? The number of bits equals the number of signal samples (44,100) times the number of seconds (1) times the number of channels (2) times the number of bits per sample (16). There are 1,411,200 bits of code for every second of music.

This digitized information is transferred to the CDs. On the disc, the code is expressed through a spiral of pits and lands. The pits are tiny holes, and the lands are flat areas that reflect the light of the laser beam. "Dark" pits represent the zeros in binary code, and "bright" lands represent the ones. The laser beam reads the pits and lands, and the information is translated back into sound

Each CD is duplicated, or copied, from a master disc. The machines that produce the copies can make one CD every five seconds, or about 720 an hour. More than a million CDs may be duplicated when a new recording by a popular group or artist is to be released.

Reading Time _____

Recalling Facts

1. CDs almost never wear out because they are
   - a. played by a needle.
   - b. made out of vinyl.
   - c. played by a beam of light.

2. The process by which a microphone captures sound waves is called
   - a. digitizing.
   - b. signal sampling.
   - c. amplitude.

3. There are _____ digits in binary code.
   - a. 10
   - b. 2
   - c. 3

4. Sounds are represented on a CD by
   - a. a spiral of pits and lands.
   - b. lines of holes and flat areas.
   - c. round grooves.

5. Each second of music on a CD uses about how many signal samples?
   - a. 16
   - b. 44,100
   - c. 1,411,200

Understanding Ideas

6. When information is digitized, it is
   - a. changed into binary code.
   - b. turned into sound.
   - c. recorded in pits and lands.

7. Music recorded using 25,000 signal samples per second would probably sound
   - a. just like a live performance.
   - b. bad or inaccurate.
   - c. extremely soft.

8. Sound separated into two channels could be described as
   - a. quadrophonic.
   - b. monophonic.
   - c. stereophonic.

9. One could conclude from this passage that "bits" of information in a computer program would refer to
   - a. the digits of binary code in the program.
   - b. the number of digits in a string of binary code.
   - c. the quality of the picture on the computer screen.

10. According to this passage, CDs may be preferable to long-playing records because
    - a. they sound better.
    - b. they last longer.
    - c. they are easier to store.

6 B Storing Compact Discs

Lynette wants to store her compilation of favorite CDs in the top drawer of her nightstand. A CD case measures 5⅝ inches by 4⅞ inches and is ⅜ inch thick. Lynette's top drawer is 15¼ inches long by 11 inches wide and is 6¼ inches deep. Lynette stores her CDs by standing the cases so that each CD's title can be easily read.

   Lynette can store the CDs in rows in two directions—down the length of the drawer or across its width. First she figures out how many CDs will fit if they are down the length of the drawer. She divides 11 by 4⅞ and finds that she can fit two CDs across, with their titles facing up. She then divides 15¼ by ⅜ and calculates that she can fit 40 CDs in a row, so she can store 80 CDs in the two rows. Lynette then calculates how many CDs will fit in the other direction. She divides 15¼ by 4⅞ and finds that she can fit three rows across. She divides 11 by ⅜ and finds that 29 CDs will fit in each row. Multiplying by three, she finds she can fit 87 CDs in this direction.

1. **Recognizing Words in Context**

   Find the word *compilation* in the passage. One definition below is closest to the meaning of that word. One definition has the opposite or nearly the opposite meaning. The remaining definition has a completely different meaning. Label the definitions C for *closest*, O for *opposite or nearly opposite*, and D for *different*.

   _____ a. gift

   _____ b. pair

   _____ c. collection

2. **Distinguishing Fact from Opinion**

   Two of the statements below present *facts*, which can be proved. The other statement is an *opinion*, which expresses someone's thoughts or beliefs. Label the statements F for *fact* and O for *opinion*.

   _____ a. Lynette should have stored her CDs in a larger drawer.

   _____ b. Lynette knew the two best ways to store her CDs.

   _____ c. Lynette stored her CDs with the titles facing up.

3. **Keeping Events in Order**

   Number the statements below 1, 2, and 3 to show the order of the steps described in the passage.

   _____ a. Compare how many CDs will fit in each direction to see which direction can hold the most.

   _____ b. Find how many CDs will fit in each direction.

   _____ c. Find the size of the storage space and of a CD case.

4. **Making Correct Inferences**

   Two of the statements below are correct *inferences,* or reasonable guesses. They are based on information in the passage. The other statement is an incorrect, or faulty, inference. Label the statements C for *correct* inference and F for *faulty* inference.

   _____ a. The depth of the top drawer is not important.

   _____ b. Being able to see the labels is more important to Lynette than the number of CDs she can store.

   _____ c. Lynette's method will not work if she stores her CDs on a shelf at eye level.

5. **Understanding Main Ideas**

   One of the statements below expresses the main idea of the passage. One statement is too general, or too broad. The other explains only part of the passage; it is too narrow. Label the statements M for *main idea,* B for *too broad,* and N for *too narrow.*

   _____ a. Storing CDs the right way requires multiplication and division.

   _____ b. There are only a few practical ways to store CDs.

   _____ c. Lynette uses math to figure out the best way to store the most CDs in a drawer.

Correct Answers, Part A _____

Correct Answers, Part B _____

Total Correct Answers _____

7 A   Calories and Health

People need energy to grow, move, and do everything in life. They eat food to gain that energy, which is measured in calories. A calorie is a unit of energy. One calorie is the amount of energy, or heat, needed to raise the temperature of 1 gram of water 1 degree Celsius. The calories on food labels are really kilocalories. A kilocalorie equals 1,000 calories. A candy bar containing 200 calories really contains 200 kilocalories, or 200,000 calories.

Food calories (cal) come from the three main parts of all foods—fat, protein, and carbohydrates (carbs). A gram of fat has 9 calories, a gram of protein has 4 calories, and a gram of carbs has 4 calories. The nutrition label on the side of a box of cereal might say that a serving has 4 grams of fat, 2 grams of protein, and 22 grams of carbs for a total of 132 calories. Of the total calories, 36 come from fat (4g × 9 cal = 36 cal), 8 from protein (2g × 4 cal = 8 cal), and 88 from carbs (22g × 4 cal = 88 cal).

Because fat contains more than twice the calories of protein and of carbs, fatty foods contain the most calories. For instance, butter, some vegetable oils, and fatty meats contain lots of fat and therefore store lots of calories. A large double-patty cheeseburger is a fatty food containing about 700 calories. Of the total calories, 393.3 come from fat (43.7g × 9 cal), 158.8 come from carbs (39.7g × 4 cal), and 152 come from protein (38.0g × 4 cal).

Everyone needs to eat about 2,000 calories each day to stay at the same weight. The number varies based on height, weight, gender, age, and activity level. The Food and Drug Administration (FDA) recommends 1,600 calories for women and 2,200 calories for men who don't get much exercise. The FDA recommends 2,200 calories for active women, such as dancers. The guideline for active men, such as football players, is 2,800 calories.

The guidelines should be adjusted until the right balance is found for each person. People keep a healthy weight by balancing the calories consumed with the calories used each day. People who eat fewer calories than they use can become too thin. People who eat more calories than they use can become obese. Small changes in diet can help people get just the right amount of energy they need each day.

Reading Time _____

Recalling Facts

1. A calorie is
   - ❏ a. a measure of fat.
   - ❏ b. 1 degree Celsius.
   - ❏ c. a unit of energy.

2. A gram of fat has
   - ❏ a. 9 calories.
   - ❏ b. 4 calories.
   - ❏ c. 1,000 calories.

3. A gram of protein or carbs has
   - ❏ a. 9 calories.
   - ❏ b. 4 calories.
   - ❏ c. 1,000 calories.

4. If you consume the same number of calories as you use each day, you will
   - ❏ a. lose weight.
   - ❏ b. maintain your weight.
   - ❏ c. gain weight.

5. If you reduce your calorie intake or raise your daily activity level, you will
   - ❏ a. lose weight.
   - ❏ b. maintain your weight.
   - ❏ c. gain weight.

Understanding Ideas

6. One can conclude from reading the passage that calories
   - ❏ a. from protein are good for you.
   - ❏ b. from fat are bad for you.
   - ❏ c. need to be regulated.

7. One can conclude from the passage that the number of calories a person needs to consume each day
   - ❏ a. is 2,000.
   - ❏ b. depends on personal factors.
   - ❏ c. increases if the person is inactive.

8. You could conclude that raising your daily calorie intake and maintaining your activity level would
   - ❏ a. cause a weight loss.
   - ❏ b. maintain your weight.
   - ❏ c. cause a weight gain.

9. According to the passage, humans eat food to gain
   - ❏ a. pleasure.
   - ❏ b. energy.
   - ❏ c. weight.

10. If one needed to add weight quickly, one would eat foods high in
    - ❏ a. fat.
    - ❏ b. protein.
    - ❏ c. carbs.

7 B Feeding Sled Dogs for the Iditarod

Each winter Alaska holds a race over a 1,150-mile trail for sled-dog racers, called mushers, and their dog teams. The race runs from Anchorage in south-central Alaska to Nome on the western coast, and it can take from 9 to 17 days.

The mushers need to make sure the dogs get enough calories every day to maintain their strength. A sled-dog team can have 16 Alaskan husky dogs, each weighing about 55 pounds. They run more than 100 miles each day, pulling a sled through several inches of snow and sometimes over rough terrain.

Before the race begins, mushers must figure out how much food their dogs will need and then send equal portions for each of them ahead to a number of checkpoints along the race path. The dogs need to consume about 10,000 calories per day, but they can't get too heavy to run. So mushers plan to feed each of the dogs four times a day with one pound of high-calorie food that stores about 2,500 calories per pound. Each musher purchases, divides, and sends ahead about 832 pounds of dog food for his or her Iditarod team. (16 dogs × 4 pounds a day × about 13 days = 832 pounds.)

1. **Recognizing Words in Context**

   Find the word *terrain* in the passage. One definition below is closest to the meaning of that word. One definition has the opposite or nearly the opposite meaning. The remaining definition has a completely different meaning. Label the definitions C for *closest*, O for *opposite or nearly opposite*, and D for *different*.

   _____ a. water
   _____ b. race
   _____ c. land

2. **Distinguishing Fact from Opinion**

   Two of the statements below present *facts*, which can be proved. The other statement is an *opinion*, which expresses someone's thoughts or beliefs. Label the statements F for *fact* and O for *opinion*.

   _____ a. A sled-dog race is the best kind of race.
   _____ b. Dogs require about 10,000 calories a day during the Iditarod.
   _____ c. Dogs pull sleds over snow and uneven land.

3. **Keeping Events in Order**

   Number the statements below 1, 2, and 3 to show the order in which the events take place.

   _____ a. Mushers buy the bulk food and divide it into equal portions.

   _____ b. Mushers figure out how much food their dogs will need.

   _____ c. The food is shipped to checkpoints.

4. **Making Correct Inferences**

   Two of the statements below are correct *inferences*, or reasonable guesses. They are based on information in the passage. The other statement is an incorrect, or faulty, inference. Label the statements C for *correct* inference and F for *faulty* inference.

   _____ a. The more difficult the terrain, the more calories dogs will burn during the race.

   _____ b. The Iditarod requires the strength of mushers and dogs.

   _____ c. Feeding the dogs twice as much daily as needed would help the dogs run faster.

5. **Understanding Main Ideas**

   One of the statements below expresses the main idea of the passage. One statement is too general, or too broad. The other explains only part of the passage; it is too narrow. Label the statements M for *main idea*, B for *too broad*, and N for *too narrow*.

   _____ a. Sled dogs require a certain number of calories per day for the Iditarod.

   _____ b. Sled dogs' food should have 2,500 calories per pound.

   _____ c. The Iditarod is a long, hard race.

Correct Answers, Part A _____

Correct Answers, Part B _____

Total Correct Answers _____

8 A Mayan Mathematics

The Mayan culture flourished in Mexico and Central America from 250 until around 900. The Maya developed a written language and a number system that included the concept of zero.

A dot and a bar were used as symbols to express numbers. Their combinations determined the values of the numbers. For numbers less than 20, a dot stood for one unit, and a bar stood for five units. Four dots, then, stood for 4, three bars stood for 15, and three dots and one bar represented 8. The smaller units were shown stacked on top of the larger ones. The number 6 was a dot on top of a bar (1 + 5). The number 19 was shown as four dots on top of three bars (4 + 15).

Numbers were counted together this way only as far as 19, because the Maya used a base-20 number system. Their system worked basically the same way as our base-10 number system. In our system, the 10 digits from 0 to 9 are combined with powers of 10 to form numbers larger than 9. In the base-20 system, the 20 symbols from 0 to 19 were combined with powers of 20. A power is a base number multiplied by itself as many times as shown in the exponent ($20 = 20^1$, $400 = 20^2$, $8,000 = 20^3$, etc.). In base-10, 34 is shown as $3 \times 10 + 4$. In base-20, 34 was shown as $1 \times 20 + 14$.

Place value in Mayan mathematics was shown by placing the higher values above the others in a column. To find the value of a number, all anyone had to do was add the dots and bars in the column, multiplying each sum by the value of its place. The place values in Mayan mathematics are the 1s place, 20s place, 400s place, 8,000s place, and so on. Mayan place values go up by powers of 20.

One unit of 20 was indicated as one dot above the units it was added to. So 23 would be a dot above three dots. What would 20 be? The zero was represented by a shell. The number 20 was shown as a dot above a shell. The number 100 was shown as a bar in the 20s place ($5 \times 20 = 100$) above a shell. The number 140 would be shown as two dots over a bar in the 20s place above a shell in the 1s place.

Reading Time _____

Recalling Facts

1. In the Mayan number system, dots and bars represented
   - ❑ a. one unit and five units.
   - ❑ b. 0 and 10.
   - ❑ c. 5s and 10s.

2. The base of the Mayan number system was
   - ❑ a. 10.
   - ❑ b. 15.
   - ❑ c. 20.

3. Combinations of symbols represented the values of numbers
   - ❑ a. 1 to 9.
   - ❑ b. 1 to 19.
   - ❑ c. 0 to 19.

4. Place value was shown by placing
   - ❑ a. higher values above the lower values.
   - ❑ b. lower values beside the higher values.
   - ❑ c. higher values below the lower values.

5. A bar in the 20s place equals
   - ❑ a. 100.
   - ❑ b. 50.
   - ❑ c. 5.

Understanding Ideas

6. A dot above a shell above another shell indicates
   - ❑ a. one place value.
   - ❑ b. two place values.
   - ❑ c. three place values.

7. One dot in each of the three places would indicate the number
   - ❑ a. 41.
   - ❑ b. 111.
   - ❑ c. 421.

8. In Mayan mathematics, the second place value is 20^2, or
   - ❑ a. $20 \times 20 \times 20$.
   - ❑ b. 20×20.
   - ❑ c. 20×2.

9. One can conclude that a shell is *not* needed
   - ❑ a. in the 20s place to show the number 20.
   - ❑ b. in the 1s place when a quantity is in the 20s place.
   - ❑ c. whenever a zero is needed.

10. One can conclude that to get the sum of two large numbers,
    - ❑ a. first find the sum of each column and add the sums for the total.
    - ❑ b. first find the sum of each place value and then add the sums for the total.
    - ❑ c. both of the above are true.

8 B Early Money

Money is whatever people agree to use in exchange for goods and services. Barter was a simple system of exchange in many early societies. Certain items were chosen as a medium of exchange for a number of reasons. They were easy to store or convenient to carry. Some items were chosen because they were durable, and they lasted a long time. Any item that was chosen to be exchanged as money had to have value for both parties.

Examples of items that were used for barter in early civilizations include cattle, sacks of grain, and animal skins and teeth. Salt was used in the Roman Empire because it could be weighed, was easily transported, and was generally rare, so it had value. Metal items were also popular forms of money. A lump of copper, for example, had a certain value assigned to it by volume or mass. Ancient Chinese people also crafted metal into miniature tools, which gave the metal a higher value for exchange.

Shells were another common form of money. Ancient civilizations in China, India, Africa, and North America all used shells for currency. Shells could be counted out singly instead of weighed like copper or handed over whole like cattle. Counting them meant that a fixed value could be assigned to each item of exchange.

1. **Recognizing Words in Context**

   Find the word *miniature* in the passage. One definition below is closest to the meaning of that word. One definition has the opposite or nearly the opposite meaning. The remaining definition has a completely different meaning. Label the definitions C for *closest,* O for *opposite or nearly opposite,* and D for *different.*

   _____ a. tiny
   _____ b. huge
   _____ c. heavy

2. **Distinguishing Fact from Opinion**

   Two of the statements below present *facts,* which can be proved. The other statement is an *opinion,* which expresses someone's thoughts or beliefs. Label the statements F for *fact* and O for *opinion.*

   _____ a. The Chinese had the most clever form of money.
   _____ b. Early civilizations in many parts of the world used shells for money.
   _____ c. Metal had a certain value assigned to it by volume and mass.

3. **Keeping Events in Order**

   Number the statements below 1, 2, and 3 to show the order in which the events were described in the passage.

   _____ a. Shells could be counted, which gave them a set value.

   _____ b. Any item that had value could be used as a medium of exchange.

   _____ c. Miniature metal tools became more highly valued than lumps of metal.

4. **Making Correct Inferences**

   Two of the statements below are correct *inferences*, or reasonable guesses. They are based on information in the passage. The other statement is an incorrect, or faulty, inference. Label the statements C for *correct* inference and F for *faulty* inference.

   _____ a. Early money differed around the world, as different peoples chose what was most valuable to them.

   _____ b. The saying that lazy workers are not "worth their salt" may date back to Roman times.

   _____ c. An item that was sturdy and easy to carry had greater value than food or cattle.

5. **Understanding Main Ideas**

   One of the statements below expresses the main idea of the passage. One statement is too general, or too broad. The other explains only part of the passage; it is too narrow. Label the statements M for *main idea*, B for *too broad*, and N for *too narrow*.

   _____ a. Salt, metal, and shells were used as early forms of money.

   _____ b. In early civilizations, items were chosen for barter on the basis of their value to both parties.

   _____ c. Money is whatever people agree to use in exchange for goods and services.

Correct Answers, Part A _____

Correct Answers, Part B _____

Total Correct Answers _____

9 A One Dimension, Two Dimension, Three Dimension, Four

In mathematics, *dimension* means "a measure of spatial extent." A straight line that extends from one point to another is one-dimensional. A rectangle is two-dimensional. A cube is three-dimensional. Dimensions can be better understood by looking at the number of measurements for each.

The first dimension begins as a straight line drawn in any direction from any point. One straight line differs from any other only by one measurement, the length. If the line were allowed to go on without end, or to infinity, it would still cover only one-dimensional space.

Drawing another line extending out from that line, at a 90-degree angle, for instance, would create a second dimension. Two-dimensional objects have width as well as length. Circles, triangles, and squares are two-dimensional because they lie on a plane that is two-dimensional. If any one of these figures were expanded infinitely in any direction, it would still cover only two-dimensional space.

Adding height to a two-dimensional object makes it three-dimensional. Think of a cube. With the addition of the third measurement—height—a square extends into the third dimension and becomes a solid. If the cube were expanded infinitely in all three directions, it would still cover only three-dimensional space. Three-dimensional objects, or solids, are familiar to us because all real objects have height, width, and length.

The fourth dimension extends the spatial properties of height, width, and length. *Tetraspace* is a term that describes the fourth dimension. If you were living in a two-dimensional world and a cube passed through your world, you'd see a square appear all of a sudden, stay a moment, and then vanish. The same would happen if a four-dimensional hypercube passed through our world. Maybe we'd see a cube appear all of a sudden, stay for a while, and then vanish. Or imagine a three-dimensional cube that moves from point A to point B. The cube moving through space from one point to another is another way to think of the fourth dimension. Other dimensions are said to exist beyond the fourth dimension.

Scientists, builders, and designers are some of the people who deal with the first, second, and third dimensions as part of their daily work. Mathematicians and physicists deal with four or more dimensions. The key to understanding the fourth dimension and beyond is the ability to use your imagination.

Reading Time _____

Recalling Facts

1. A measure of spatial extent is called
   - a. tetraspace.
   - b. a dimension.
   - c. infinity.

2. A triangle is
   - a. one-dimensional.
   - b. two-dimensional.
   - c. three-dimensional.

3. A _____ is three-dimensional because it has height, width, and length.
   - a. square
   - b. cube
   - c. triangle

4. A two-dimensional object becomes a solid by adding
   - a. an angle.
   - b. weight.
   - c. height.

5. *Tetraspace* is a term that describes
   - a. the second dimension.
   - b. the third dimension.
   - c. the fourth dimension.

Understanding Ideas

6. One can conclude from the passage that
   - a. there actually is no fourth dimension.
   - b. we live in a two-dimensional world.
   - c. a fifth dimension would include elements of all four other dimensions.

7. A circle drawn on a sheet of paper is an example of a
   - a. two-dimensional object.
   - b. three-dimensional object.
   - c. four-dimensional object.

8. Images on a movie screen are
   - a. two-dimensional.
   - b. three-dimensional.
   - c. four-dimensional.

9. One might conclude that the fourth dimension would be an important area of study for people who
   - a. carve or mold geometrical shapes.
   - b. study earth and rocks.
   - c. study outer space.

10. By adding one dimension to a square
    - a. it becomes a cube.
    - b. it moves into tetraspace.
    - c. it becomes a triangle.

9 B Caliper for Sculpting

Samantha has signed up for a class in sculpting. Her first assignment is to make a copy of a 14-inch model of someone jogging. How closely her sculpture matches the model, including its measurements, will determine her grade.

Samantha will need to use a tool called a caliper to measure the model accurately. A caliper is used to measure the outer dimensions, inner dimensions, and depths of three-dimensional objects, especially unevenly shaped objects. A caliper looks like a cross between a ruler and a plumber's wrench.

Samantha begins by measuring the diameter of the body parts. The diameter is the length of a straight line passing through the center of an object. Samantha closes the jaws of the caliper to the width of first one leg and then the other. The diameter of each leg tapers from 1½ inches at the top to three-fourths of an inch near the foot. The head measures 1¼ inches wide, 1¾ inches from front to back, and 2¼ inches from the chin to the top. Samantha spends more time gathering as many measurements as she can. As she works the clay, she uses her caliper to measure her work. Then she compares these measurements with those of the model.

1. **Recognizing Words in Context**

   Find the word *tapers* in the passage. One definition below is closest to the meaning of that word. One definition has the opposite or nearly the opposite meaning. The remaining definition has a completely different meaning. Label the definitions C for *closest*, O for *opposite or nearly opposite*, and D for *different*.

   _____ a. widens

   _____ b. passes

   _____ c. gets thinner

2. **Distinguishing Fact from Opinion**

   Two of the statements below present *facts*, which can be proved. The other statement is an *opinion*, which expresses someone's thoughts or beliefs. Label the statements F for *fact* and O for *opinion*.

   _____ a. A caliper is used to measure three-dimensional objects.

   _____ b. Samantha could have made a good copy without using the caliper.

   _____ c. A caliper is a measuring instrument.

3. **Keeping Events in Order**

   Number the statements below 1, 2, and 3 to show the order in which the events took place.

   _____ a. Samantha measured the model's legs.

   _____ b. Samantha measured the model's head.

   _____ c. Samantha compared the measurements of her sculpture with those of the model.

4. **Making Correct Inferences**

   Two of the statements below are correct *inferences,* or reasonable guesses. They are based on information in the passage. The other statement is an incorrect, or faulty, inference. Label the statements C for *correct* inference and F for *faulty* inference.

   _____ a. A caliper can be used for measuring the inner diameter of a pipe.

   _____ b. A caliper would be used for measuring the length of the sides of a square.

   _____ c. Samantha could make a larger figure by adding the same amount to each measurement from the caliper.

5. **Understanding Main Ideas**

   One of the statements below expresses the main idea of the passage. One statement is too general, or too broad. The other explains only part of the passage; it is too narrow. Label the statements M for *main idea,* B for *too broad,* and N for *too narrow.*

   _____ a. Sculptors sometimes use a measuring tool called a caliper.

   _____ b. A caliper has "jaws" like a plumber's wrench.

   _____ c. A caliper is a tool for measuring three-dimensional, unevenly shaped objects.

Correct Answers, Part A _____

Correct Answers, Part B _____

Total Correct Answers _____

10 A The Sounds in Music

Music is a pattern of sounds or notes. Some are made one at a time, but they can be sounded together in groups called chords. Musical traditions vary greatly between cultures, but mathematical relationships between notes are constant.

Sound is a form of energy. The musical pitch of each note—whether it is high or low—is determined by its frequency. This is the speed at which its sound waves travel through air. Frequency is measured in hertz units (Hz). A frequency twice as fast as another produces the same sound at a higher pitch, and the distance, or interval, between these notes is called an octave. The A above middle C, for instance, vibrates at 440 Hz. The A an octave below it vibrates at 220 Hz; the A an octave above at 880 Hz.

An octave includes a scale. Although a scale contains only eight specific notes, an octave has 13 possible notes. The notes are a half-step apart. The frequencies of notes a half-step apart are very similar, and the sound of these notes played together can be jarring. The best way to understand a scale's half-steps is to visualize a piano keyboard. White and black keys that are side by side are a half-step apart. Two white keys not separated by a black key are also a half-step apart.

Some chords sound particularly pleasing because of the mathematical relationship between the frequencies of their notes. In any scale, the first and third notes played together produce a pleasant sound. So do the first and fourth notes, and the first and fifth notes. Notes one and three produce a chord called a third. Fourths and fifths—notes one and four, and one and five—are also attractive.

A musical key is named for the note that begins its scale. In the key of C major, the notes of the scale are C, D, E, F, G, A, B, and C. These are all white keys on a piano. E and F (notes three and four), and B and C (notes seven and eight) are a half-step apart, but the rest of the intervals are whole steps. The scales in all major keys follow the same pattern of half-steps and whole steps. The scale in a minor key follows a slightly different pattern. Notes three, six, and seven are lowered a half-step in a minor scale. Music in minor keys often sounds sad or eerie.

Reading Time _____

Recalling Facts

1. The speed at which sound waves travel through air is called
   - a. pitch.
   - b. energy.
   - c. frequency.

2. The distance between any two musical notes is
   - a. an interval.
   - b. a scale.
   - c. an octave.

3. A frequency twice as fast as another frequency produces
   - a. the same note an octave lower.
   - b. the same note an octave higher.
   - c. the same note in the same octave.

4. There are _____ notes in a scale.
   - a. 3
   - b. 8
   - c. 13

5. Sound is a form of
   - a. energy.
   - b. pitch.
   - c. culture.

Understanding Ideas

6. Music that goes with a scary movie would most likely be written in
   - a. a major key.
   - b. a minor key.
   - c. the key of C.

7. In the key of C major, the notes C and G produce which chord?
   - a. a third
   - b. a fourth
   - c. a fifth

8. Because the middle E on a piano vibrates at about 330 Hz, the E an octave below middle E would vibrate at
   - a. 165 Hz.
   - b. 322 Hz.
   - c. 660 Hz.

9. One can conclude from this passage that the faster the frequency of a sound,
   - a. the lower the pitch of the note.
   - b. the louder the sound of the note.
   - c. the higher the pitch of the note.

10. One can infer from this passage that some octaves have
    - a. more than eight notes.
    - b. more than 13 notes.
    - c. all minor notes.

10 B Kate Adebola Okikiolu

Kate Okikiolu is a professor of mathematics at the University of California, San Diego. In 1997 Okikiolu became the first African American to win the Sloan Research Fellowship award. This is the most prestigious award in mathematics research in the United States. Okikiolu studies a special branch of geometry in which she explores the properties of different dimensions in space.

Okikiolu's research included studying the sound made by a drum. She has studied a number called the "spectral determinant." This number results when all of the frequencies of a booming drum are recorded and multiplied together. The frequency of a drum sound is the number of cycles that a sound wave completes in a given time. Frequency is measured in hertz (Hz) units, or cycles per second. One drum may have a frequency of 110.00 Hz. But another drum of a different shape—but perhaps not a larger one—may have a frequency eight times higher at 880.00 Hz.

Using mathematics, Okikiolu can determine the sound a drum will make by its shape. Other people have understood the spectral determinant of a two-dimensional drum skin. But no one before Okikiolu applied it to the three-dimensional space of the whole drum, which includes the sound box as well as the drum skin.

1. **Recognizing Words in Context**

   Find the word *prestigious* in the passage. One definition below is closest to the meaning of that word. One definition has the opposite or nearly the opposite meaning. The remaining definition has a completely different meaning. Label the definitions C for *closest*, O for *opposite or nearly opposite*, and D for *different*.

   _____ a. minor
   _____ b. costly
   _____ c. important

2. **Distinguishing Fact from Opinion**

   Two of the statements below present *facts,* which can be proved. The other statement is an *opinion,* which expresses someone's thoughts or beliefs. Label the statements F for *fact* and O for *opinion*.

   _____ a. Two drums of the same size may give off different frequencies.
   _____ b. The number of cycles that a sound wave completes in a given time is its frequency.
   _____ c. A drum with a higher frequency produces a more pleasing sound.

3. **Keeping Events in Order**

   Number the statements below 1, 2, and 3 to show the order in which the events take place.

   _____ a. Each frequency of the booming drum is recorded.

   _____ b. A drum is struck, causing many frequencies.

   _____ c. All frequencies are multiplied to reveal the spectral determinant.

4. **Making Correct Inferences**

   Two of the statements below are correct *inferences,* or reasonable guesses. They are based on information in the passage. The other statement is an incorrect, or faulty, inference. Label the statements C for *correct* inference and F for *faulty* inference.

   _____ a. Different-shaped drums create different spectral determinants.

   _____ b. Square drums produce the same frequencies as round drums.

   _____ c. Different-sized drums create different frequencies.

5. **Understanding Main Ideas**

   One of the statements below expresses the main idea of the passage. One statement is too general, or too broad. The other explains only part of the passage; it is too narrow. Label the statements M for *main idea,* B for *too broad,* and N for *too narrow.*

   _____ a. When struck, a drum produces many frequencies.

   _____ b. Okikiolu developed a mathematical way to determine the sound a drum will make.

   _____ c. Kate Okikiolu is a professor who studies a special branch of geometry.

Correct Answers, Part A _____

Correct Answers, Part B _____

Total Correct Answers _____

11 A   A History of Measuring Systems

In ancient times, people did not need precise units of measure. They used parts of their bodies to measure length and distance. They counted seeds to measure volume and weight. But as cultures advanced, people needed more complex measuring systems. They needed an accurate one. They wanted one in which measurements were standard and meant the same thing to every user.

An early standardized system of measure was the English imperial system. A form of it is still in use today. The foot, pound, and quart are units of measure in this system. The base numbers used, such as 12 inches for 1 foot and 16 ounces for 1 pound, make it difficult, however, to do complex calculations.

In the early 19th century, France designed a new system of measure called the metric system. Its units of measure are the meter, the gram, and the liter. The metric system is a decimal system, which means that all the units of measure are multiples of 10. This system made complex calculations easier. Today almost all nations have adopted the modern metric system.

Although the United States has permitted the use of the metric system since 1866, the nation still relies on a form of the English system in daily life. Those in business and science fields most often use the metric system at work. But the U.S. public still prefers the traditional system.

Many people must work with both systems on a daily basis. For example, an engineer might use the metric system to design city plans. On the other hand, a construction worker on a city project might use the traditional system. If the engineer's plan calls for 40 meters of underground pipe, the worker needs to convert meters to yards and then feet because the pipe is measured in feet. There are 1.09 yards in a meter. Multiplying 40 meters by 1.09 tells how many yards are in 40 meters. Forty meters is the same as 43.6 yards. There are 3 feet in a yard, so the worker will need 130.8 feet of pipe.

Because using multiple systems is so complicated, there is a push toward exclusive use of the metric system in Europe. Distances and speeds on road signs and car speedometers in Ireland are now expressed in kilometers instead of miles. By 2009 all product labels in Europe will show only metric measures. In the United States, however, the government has neither required nor restricted the use of either system.

Reading Time _____

Recalling Facts

1. The foot, pound, and quart are units of measure in
   - ❏ a. the French system.
   - ❏ b. the modern metric system.
   - ❏ c. the English imperial system.

2. The units of measure in the metric system are
   - ❏ a. the meter, gram, and liter.
   - ❏ b. body parts and seeds.
   - ❏ c. the inch, foot, and yard.

3. All the units of measure are multiples of 10
   - ❏ a. in a decimal system.
   - ❏ b. in the English system.
   - ❏ c. in early measurement systems.

4. One meter is equal to
   - ❏ a. 3 quarts.
   - ❏ b. 12 inches.
   - ❏ c. 1.09 yards.

5. There is a push toward exclusive use of the metric system in
   - ❏ a. Europe.
   - ❏ b. the United States.
   - ❏ c. India.

Understanding Ideas

6. One can conclude from the passage that the United States
   - ❏ a. has not yet adopted the metric system.
   - ❏ b. uses a measurement system that no other nation uses.
   - ❏ c. does not favor exclusive use of the metric system.

7. Which of the following road signs would most likely be found in the United States?
   - ❏ a. Next Exit 500 Yards
   - ❏ b. Reduce Speed 200 Meters
   - ❏ c. Speed Limit 100 Kilometers Per Hour

8. Which of the following is most likely to be on a product label in a nation that uses the metric system?
   - ❏ a. Net Wt. 500 grams
   - ❏ b. Net Wt. 1.5 pounds
   - ❏ c. Volume 1 quart

9. One can conclude that using two measuring systems in a nation
   - ❏ a. improves the accuracy of measurements.
   - ❏ b. can cause problems in some fields.
   - ❏ c. is a growing international trend.

10. One can infer from the passage that converting a value from one set of units to another, if done correctly, results in
    - ❏ a. a larger value.
    - ❏ b. an equivalent value.
    - ❏ c. an inaccurate value.

11 B Miles Versus Kilometers

Jin is driving from Syracuse, New York, to Quebec City in Canada to visit his aunt. She sent him a distance chart with the distances measured in kilometers because Canada uses the metric system.

In Watertown, New York, Jin stops to check his progress. He sees from his chart that there are still 40 kilometers to the border, where Highway 401 will take him to Quebec City. Jin knows he can convert kilometers to miles by multiplying by 0.6 and miles to kilometers by dividing by 0.6 (that's about the same as multiplying by 1.67, or ⅔). He multiplies 40 by 0.6 and finds that there are 24 miles to the border.

Driving on Highway 401, Jin sees that his gas gauge is on empty. He guesses he can travel perhaps 15 more miles before he runs out of gas. A billboard says it's 20 kilometers to the next gas station. Jin nervously multiplies 15 by ⅔ and is quickly reassured that he can drive 25 kilometers more.

While driving through Montreal at about 2:00 P.M., Jin wonders when he'll arrive in Quebec City. He knows that Quebec City is about 165 miles from Montreal. The speed limit is 100 kilometers per hour the rest of the way. Jin multiplies 100 × 0.6 to get 60 miles per hour. He divides 165 by 60 and figures he'll arrive around 4:45.

1. **Recognizing Words in Context**

   Find the word *reassured* in the passage. One definition below is closest to the meaning of that word. One definition has the opposite or nearly the opposite meaning. The remaining definition has a completely different meaning. Label the definitions C for *closest*, O for *opposite or nearly opposite*, and D for *different*.

   _____ a. worried
   _____ b. relieved
   _____ c. interested

2. **Distinguishing Fact from Opinion**

   Two of the statements below present *facts*, which can be proved. The other statement is an *opinion*, which expresses someone's thoughts or beliefs. Label the statements F for *fact* and O for *opinion*.

   _____ a. Distance charts should include only metric measurements.
   _____ b. The highway speed limit between Montreal and Quebec City converts to 60 miles per hour.
   _____ c. The U.S. and Canada use different systems for measuring distance.

3. **Keeping Events in Order**

   Number the statements below 1, 2, and 3 to show the order in which the events took place.

   _____ a. Jin calculated the number of miles to the next gas station.

   _____ b. Jin realized his car was almost out of gas.

   _____ c. Jin began driving along Highway 401 in Canada.

4. **Making Correct Inferences**

   Two of the statements below are correct *inferences,* or reasonable guesses. They are based on information in the passage. The other statement is an incorrect, or faulty, inference. Label the statements C for *correct* inference and F for *faulty* inference.

   _____ a. A person can drive from Syracuse to Quebec City in one day.

   _____ b. Highway 401 to Quebec City begins near the U.S.–Canada border, north of Watertown, New York.

   _____ c. Jin would not have made it to the gas station if he had not calculated the distance correctly.

5. **Understanding Main Ideas**

   One of the statements below expresses the main idea of the passage. One statement is too general, or too broad. The other explains only part of the passage; it is too narrow. Label the statements M for *main idea,* B for *too broad,* and N for *too narrow.*

   _____ a. Jin used his knowledge of converting measurements to help him travel to Quebec City, Canada.

   _____ b. It's about 165 miles from Montreal to Quebec City.

   _____ c. One can convert miles to kilometers and kilometers to miles using the decimal fraction 0.6.

Correct Answers, Part A _____

Correct Answers, Part B _____

Total Correct Answers _____

12 A   Weight Limits in Trucking

The federal government sets weight limits on how much a truck can haul safely and on how the weight is to be distributed among the truck's axles. A tractor-trailer truck typically has five axles. There are three on the cab and two on the trailer. Axle 1 is at the front of the cab. Axles 2 and 3 are paired at the rear of the cab. Axles 4 and 5 are paired on the trailer.

Federal weight limits apply to gross vehicle weight as well as to the weight on each axle. Gross vehicle weight is the weight of the truck plus its load. The limit is 80,000 pounds. The weight on a single axle is limited to 20,000 pounds. The weight on paired axles is limited to 34,000 pounds. Here is an example of weight limits for a tractor-trailer. Axle 1 under the cab of the truck supports 11,000 pounds, and each set of tandem axles supports 34,000 pounds. The weight on the axles is within the limits, and the gross vehicle weight does not exceed the limit of 80,000 pounds (11,000 + 34,000 + 34,000 = 79,000). This truck is safe for operation.

Axle weight limits exist to make sure the gross vehicle weight is evenly distributed. A tractor-trailer's center of gravity is the point about which the weight of the truck is balanced. The wheelbase of a tractor-trailer is the distance from the front axle to the centerline of the rear axles. The wheelbase determines in part where the truck's center of gravity is. For example, the shorter the wheelbase, the greater the weight resting on the rear axles. A longer wheelbase spreads a load more evenly among a truck's axles.

When loading a truck, the driver must be sure to spread the load evenly. For example, a driver wants to load a backhoe and a tractor on a flatbed trailer. The backhoe weighs 15,000 pounds, and the tractor weighs 36,500 pounds. If the driver loads the backhoe onto the front of the trailer and the tractor onto the rear, the load will exceed the weight limit for the rear axles. Subtracting 34,000 pounds from 36,500 pounds shows that the weight will exceed the limit by 2,500 pounds. The heavier equipment at the rear will shift the center of gravity too far back. The rear axles will have to carry too much of the load. The weight of the truck will not be in balance, and the truck will be unsafe. If the driver loads the tractor onto the front, however, the problem will be solved. The weight of the tractor will be more evenly distributed among the axles.

Reading Time _____

Recalling Facts

1. The federal government sets rules for how much weight a truck can haul and for
   - a. how many axles it has.
   - b. how the weight is distributed.
   - c. how long it is.

2. A typical tractor-trailer truck has
   - a. two axles.
   - b. five axles.
   - c. eight axles.

3. The gross vehicle weight limit for a tractor-trailer truck is
   - a. 20,000 pounds.
   - b. 34,000 pounds.
   - c. 80,000 pounds.

4. The point about which the weight of a truck is balanced is the
   - a. wheelbase.
   - b. center of gravity.
   - c. gross vehicle weight.

5. Heavy equipment at the rear of a trailer shifts the center of gravity to the
   - a. back.
   - b. front.
   - c. side.

Understanding Ideas

6. According to the passage, one could conclude that a trailer load should be
   - a. supported mostly by the front axles.
   - b. evenly distributed across the truck's axles.
   - c. supported mostly by the rear axles.

7. From the passage, one could conclude that trucks that exceed gross vehicle weight limits are
   - a. poorly loaded.
   - b. well-balanced.
   - c. unsafe for operation.

8. A truck that has a single-axle weight of 20,000 pounds and a weight of 38,000 pounds per paired axle is
   - a. below the weight limit.
   - b. at the weight limit.
   - c. above the weight limit.

9. From the passage, one could conclude that weight limits are
   - a. too restrictive.
   - b. inconsistently enforced.
   - c. important for safety.

10. Loading heavier cargo toward the front of a trailer shifts the center of gravity
    - a. away from the rear of the trailer.
    - b. toward the rear of the trailer.
    - c. to the front of the cab.

12 B Independent Truckers: Contracting with Trucking Companies

An owner-operator is a trucker who buys a tractor-trailer rig and contracts with trucking companies to haul trailer loads. Lee is an owner-operator, and he needs to figure out which of the following jobs pays the most.

Companies A and B pay truckers a percentage of the profit they earn from a haul. Company A pays 85 percent of its profit to the trucker. The company averages a profit of about $1.00 per mile, so Lee would earn 85 cents per mile with Company A ($1.00 × .85 = 85 cents). Company B pays 75 percent of its profit. The company averages a profit of about $1.20 per mile, so Lee would earn 90 cents per mile with Company B ($1.20 × .75 = 90 cents). Lee would earn more per mile with Company B.

But Lee needs to consider other factors. The mileage for each trip is approximately the same, so that would not affect his pay. Another issue is deadhead miles, the number of miles a trucker must travel without a load. Company B compensates for miles only when the trucker is hauling a load. If Lee were not able to secure a load from another company to haul back, he would earn nothing for his return trip. Company A, however, pays 65 cents per deadhead mile. Lee decides to contract with Company A.

1. **Recognizing Words in Context**

   Find the word *compensates* in the passage. One definition below is closest to the meaning of that word. One definition has the opposite or nearly the opposite meaning. The remaining definition has a completely different meaning. Label the definitions C for *closest*, O for *opposite or nearly opposite*, and D for *different*.

   _____ a. receives

   _____ b. pays

   _____ c. agrees

2. **Distinguishing Fact from Opinion**

   Two of the statements below present *facts*, which can be proved. The other statement is an *opinion*, which expresses someone's thoughts or beliefs. Label the statements F for *fact* and O for *opinion*.

   _____ a. Pay for a truck driver varies.

   _____ b. Most truck drivers are rich.

   _____ c. Owner-operators contract with trucking companies.

3. **Keeping Events in Order**

   Number the statements below 1, 2, and 3 to show the order in which the events take place.

   _____ a. Lee buys a tractor-trailer rig.

   _____ b. Lee decides to take the job with Company A.

   _____ c. Lee calculates which job would pay more.

4. **Making Correct Inferences**

   Two of the statements below are correct *inferences,* or reasonable guesses. They are based on information in the passage. The other statement is an incorrect, or faulty, inference. Label the statements C for *correct* inference and F for *faulty* inference.

   _____ a. Company B makes more money per mile than Company A.

   _____ b. An owner-operator's income is steady.

   _____ c. Lee contracts with Company A because he would earn more.

5. **Understanding Main Ideas**

   One of the statements below expresses the main idea of the passage. One statement is too general, or too broad. The other explains only part of the passage; it is too narrow. Label the statements M for *main idea,* B for *too broad,* and N for *too narrow.*

   _____ a. Lee has a trucking business.

   _____ b. Lee decides between two contracts with trucking companies.

   _____ c. Lee calculates his pay per mile for two companies.

Correct Answers, Part A _____

Correct Answers, Part B _____

Total Correct Answers _____

13 A — Different Ways of Counting

Numbers represent groups of things. Pretend you have three mangoes. You can say, "I have a mango, a mango, and a mango," but you can also say, "I have three mangoes." The number 3 is a symbol representing three things. Similarly, the number 10 is a symbol for 10 things. This symbol means there is one group of 10 things and nothing—zero—in addition to that.

Our counting system is a "base-10" counting system; there are separate symbols for numbers only up to 9. Another name for the base-10 system is the decimal system. The word *decimal* is related to the Latin word *decem* and the Greek word *deka*, both of which mean "ten."

Counting systems can use any base number. In a base-6 system, for instance, there are numbers for groups containing zero to five things. The symbol for a group of six things is 10. An 11 in base-6 equals a 7 in base-10.

Why do we use the decimal system? The best explanation is that almost all people have 10 fingers. We can count easily to 10—the number represented by two hands. Ten is therefore the basic unit for expressing larger numbers. We think of 20 as two groups of 10, for instance, and 100 as 10 groups of 10.

Have humans always depended on the decimal or base-10 system? Not at all. In fact, ancient Egyptians used both base-10 and base-12 systems. In the base-10 system, they had different symbols for each group of 10: 10 was represented by a circle, 100 by a coiled rope, and 1,000 by a lotus blossom. One million, the Egyptians' largest number, was shown by the figure of a man whose arms were spread wide in amazement.

The ancient Egyptians also used a base-12 system. Instead of counting on whole fingers, they counted on the *joints* of their fingers. If you take your thumb and point first to the base of your index finger on the same hand, then to the middle joint, and then to the top joint, you can count 1, 2, 3. Move to the next finger and you can count 4, 5, 6, and the third and fourth fingers continue, 7, 8, 9 and 10, 11, 12. By using both hands, the Egyptians counted up to 24. It was the ancient Egyptians who divided the day into 24 hours.

Reading Time _____

Recalling Facts

1. The system we commonly use for counting is a
   - ❏ a. base-6 system.
   - ❏ b. base-10 system.
   - ❏ c. base-12 system.

2. In a base-6 system, the number 6 is written as
   - ❏ a. 1.
   - ❏ b. 6.
   - ❏ c. 10.

3. In the ancient Egyptian decimal number system, a coiled rope equaled the number
   - ❏ a. 10.
   - ❏ b. 100.
   - ❏ c. 1,000.

4. Ancient Egyptians developed a base-12 system by counting on
   - ❏ a. their thumbs.
   - ❏ b. their hands and feet.
   - ❏ c. the joints of their fingers.

5. The word *decimal* is related to a word in ancient
   - ❏ a. Greek.
   - ❏ b. Egyptian.
   - ❏ c. English.

Understanding Ideas

6. The number 8 in a base-6 system is written as
   - ❏ a. 2.
   - ❏ b. 12.
   - ❏ c. 22.

7. One can conclude from the information in this passage that the base-10 system
   - ❏ a. is a very modern way to count.
   - ❏ b. is less common than other counting systems.
   - ❏ c. has been used by many civilizations.

8. If one were to use a base-8 system of counting, the number 8 would be represented by the symbol
   - ❏ a. 8.
   - ❏ b. 9.
   - ❏ c. 10.

9. If one were to use a base-12 system, it would be necessary to invent symbols for the
   - ❏ a. ideas 10 and 11.
   - ❏ b. ideas 11 and 12.
   - ❏ c. idea of numbers.

10. If we called the base-10 system the "two-hands system," we could call base-5
    - ❏ a. the "half-hand system."
    - ❏ b. the "one-hand system."
    - ❏ c. the "fingers system."

13 B Organizing Information by the Numbers

Melvil Dewey invented his Decimal Classification System in 1876 as a way to organize all knowledge. The Dewey Decimal System is still the most commonly used way of arranging materials in public and school libraries. Each item—a book or magazine, a video or DVD—is assigned a unique call number based on its subject matter.

Dewey placed all knowledge in 10 major categories or classes: 000, for instance, is for "generalities," 500 is for "natural sciences and math," and 900 is for "history and geography." Each class is divided into 10 subclasses. For example, mathematics (510), astronomy (520), and chemistry (540) all fall under natural sciences and math. These subclasses are divided into 10 even smaller sections. The call number 523 identifies books about "specific celestial bodies."

Most Dewey numbers include a decimal point. Numbers to the right of the decimal point provide more detailed information about the subject of a book. For example, all books on stars, planets, and moons start with the number 523. What if one wants to research a particular star, say the Sun? Books numbered 523.7 are about the Sun. Books with the call number 523.76 discuss the inside of the Sun. Dewey call numbers can also include letters from an author's name and the date a book was published.

1. **Recognizing Words in Context**

   Find the word *celestial* in the passage. One definition below is closest to the meaning of that word. One definition has the opposite or nearly the opposite meaning. The remaining definition has a completely different meaning. Label the definitions C for *closest,* O for *opposite or nearly opposite,* and D for *different.*

   _____ a. heavenly
   _____ b. earthly
   _____ c. visible

2. **Distinguishing Fact from Opinion**

   Two of the statements below present *facts,* which can be proved. The other statement is an *opinion,* which expresses someone's thoughts or beliefs. Label the statements F for *fact* and O for *opinion.*

   _____ a. The Dewey Decimal System is the best way to organize library books.

   _____ b. The Dewey Decimal System divides each major category into 10 smaller categories.

   _____ c. The Dewey Decimal System can be used for all library materials.

3. **Keeping Events in Order**

   Number the statements below 1, 2, and 3 to show the order in which Dewey Decimal call numbers are created for a book.

   _____ a. The book is assigned to one of 10 subclasses based on its topic.

   _____ b. The book is assigned to one of the 10 major categories of knowledge.

   _____ c. Numbers are added to the right of the decimal point as the subject is categorized more specifically.

4. **Making Correct Inferences**

   Two of the statements below are correct *inferences,* or reasonable guesses. They are based on information in the passage. The other statement is an incorrect, or faulty, inference. Label the statements C for *correct* inference and F for *faulty* inference.

   _____ a. Numbers to the left of the decimal point in the Dewey Classification System indicate the broader subject category.

   _____ b. Walk into any library and you'll probably find the Dewey Decimal System in use.

   _____ c. The Dewey Decimal System is the only organizational system used by public libraries.

5. **Understanding Main Ideas**

   One of the statements below expresses the main idea of the passage. One statement is too general, or too broad. The other explains only part of the passage; it is too narrow. Label the statements M for *main idea,* B for *too broad,* and N for *too narrow.*

   _____ a. Libraries organize their books and other materials by subject matter.

   _____ b. Melvil Dewey invented his Decimal Classification System in 1876.

   _____ c. The Dewey Decimal System uses numbers in groups of 10 to organize library materials by subject.

Correct Answers, Part A _____

Correct Answers, Part B _____

Total Correct Answers _____

14 A   Planning and Calculating for Making Textiles

Textile workers weave fibers together to make fabrics, blankets, rugs, scarves, and clothing. The process of creating textiles involves planning and calculations. First, textile workers must calculate dimensions, design a pattern, and determine the quantity of fiber needed. Then they set a loom and begin weaving their product.

Soraya is a member of a small weaving cooperative that sells its goods throughout the state of Maine. Together, the group members bought several looms and rented a storefront in their busy tourist town. In addition to selling their goods, the members weave baby blankets and donate them to orphanages around the world.

As the tourist season ends and winter nears, Soraya begins work on a new baby blanket. The blanket will be 48 inches long by 36 inches wide. She decides on a pattern of alternating one-inch bands of pale blue and yellow.

Soraya needs to determine whether she has enough of each color yarn for the project. She will need 16 strands of yarn per inch for the warp, the vertical threads attached to the loom. The blanket will be 36 inches wide, so Soraya will need 36×16 strands, or 576 strands. Each strand will need to be longer than the blanket, about 60 inches or 5 feet long, to adhere to the loom. She will need a total of 576×5 feet, or 2,880 feet of yarn, for the warp.

Soraya knows that she usually needs about double this amount for the weft, the yarns she will weave horizontally through the warp. She will need $2 \times 2,880$ feet, or 5,760 feet, for the weft. Soraya adds the amount needed for the warp and the weft to find the total amount of yarn she needs. Then she divides this quantity by two to determine how much of each color is needed. She examines the spools of each color yarn and determines that she has enough of each color fiber to continue.

Soraya sets her loom and begins the weaving process. She carefully counts each row she weaves to keep the alternating bands of color symmetrical. The pattern she has chosen is not complicated, so she finishes the project quickly. For her next project, she decides she will create a more complex design, which will require more complicated calculations in its planning and execution.

Reading Time _____

Recalling Facts

1. Textile workers weave
   - a. nets and hammocks.
   - b. fabrics, blankets, rugs, and clothing.
   - c. baskets and straw mats.

2. The baby blanket Soraya made is
   - a. 6 feet by 8 feet.
   - b. 24 inches by 60 inches.
   - c. 48 inches by 36 inches.

3. The vertical threads attached to the loom are
   - a. the warp threads.
   - b. the shortest threads.
   - c. the weft threads.

4. The weft yarns are
   - a. set vertically.
   - b. woven through the warp yarns.
   - c. adhered to the loom.

5. A more complex textile design requires
   - a. more thread.
   - b. a larger loom.
   - c. more complicated calculations.

Understanding Ideas

6. One can conclude from the passage that a weaver's principal tool is
   - a. a ruler.
   - b. a loom.
   - c. a spinning wheel.

7. One can infer from the passage that a cooperative is
   - a. an individual's small business.
   - b. a group-owned and -operated business.
   - c. a social club.

8. If Soraya had chosen to use four colors in her design instead of two, she would have needed
   - a. less blue and yellow yarn.
   - b. more blue and yellow yarn.
   - c. the same amount of blue and yellow yarn.

9. In her calculations for the project, Soraya did not use
   - a. multiplication.
   - b. addition.
   - c. subtraction.

10. The main idea of this passage is that
    - a. weaving textiles requires planning and calculations.
    - b. cooperatives sell and donate their woven products.
    - c. textiles are functional works of art.

14 B Navajo Woven Rugs

Navajo textiles developed in the 1600s after the Pueblo people taught the Navajos to weave. Navajo weavers introduced their own designs to the art. They found that they did not always have to run the wefts through all of the warps in a weaving. This meant that the Navajo weavers could create geometric designs other than the typical horizontal bands of color. They could make diamonds, stepped triangles, and zigzags in their works.

   Navajo weavers today are known for the geometric designs in their rugs. Before a loom is even set, a weaver figures out a pattern on a grid. As weavers work, they must count where they are on the grid and perform the right action point by point. Weavers must keep track of which yarn to use. They must also keep careful count of the warps. To maintain the symmetry of the design, the weavers must be sure to add or subtract the same number of warps to pass the wefts through at each row. If 10 warps are subtracted from the weft on the left side of a stepped triangle, 10 warps must also be subtracted from the right side.

1. **Recognizing Words in Context**

   Find the word *symmetry* in the passage. One definition below is closest to the meaning of that word. One definition has the opposite or nearly the opposite meaning. The remaining definition has a completely different meaning. Label the definitions C for *closest*, O for *opposite or nearly opposite*, and D for *different*.

   _____ a. balanced design

   _____ b. uneven pattern

   _____ c. textured feel

2. **Distinguishing Fact from Opinion**

   Two of the statements below present *facts*, which can be proved. The other statement is an *opinion*, which expresses someone's thoughts or beliefs. Label the statements F for *fact* and O for *opinion*.

   _____ a. Navajo rugs are the most beautiful ever woven.

   _____ b. The Navajo weavers reached a new understanding of the use of warp and weft.

   _____ c. Early Navajo weavers used only horizontal bands of color in their textile designs.

3. **Keeping Events in Order**

   Number the statements below 1, 2, and 3 to show the order in which the events take place in rug weaving.

   _____ a. The weaver sets a loom with thread to prepare to weave.

   _____ b. The weaver plans the design, usually on a grid.

   _____ c. The weaver checks the weaving actions against the rug design.

4. **Making Correct Inferences**

   Two of the statements below are correct *inferences,* or reasonable guesses. They are based on information in the passage. The other statement is an incorrect, or faulty, inference. Label the statements C for *correct* inference and F for *faulty* inference.

   _____ a. Symmetry is important to the design of Navajo rugs.

   _____ b. Knowledge of how to form shapes is important in designing rug patterns.

   _____ c. Weaving is something that can be done while you are paying attention to other things.

5. **Understanding Main Ideas**

   One of the statements below expresses the main idea of the passage. One statement is too general, or too broad. The other explains only part of the passage; it is too narrow. Label the statements M for *main idea,* B for *too broad,* and N for *too narrow.*

   _____ a. The Pueblo people introduced weaving to the Navajos.

   _____ b. Navajo rug design requires careful planning and calculations.

   _____ c. Math is useful in any weaving project.

   Correct Answers, Part A _____

   Correct Answers, Part B _____

   Total Correct Answers _____

15 A Paying for the Civil War

The Civil War (1861–65) was by far the most costly war the United States had fought up to that point in history. Whereas the Mexican War (1846–48) had cost about $70 million, the Civil War cost about $3 billion. The federal government was able to borrow some of the funds it needed. To raise more money, the government passed the Revenue Act of 1862. The major outcome of this act was the creation of the federal income tax.

Compared with modern income tax laws, the 1862 Revenue Act was simple. The yearly tax rate was 3 percent on incomes from $600 to $10,000. Incomes of more than $10,000 were taxed at 5 percent. Taxable income was defined as wages, salaries, interest, and dividends. The law also specified that in some special cases, the payment of additional taxes was required.

Here is an example of how an average American citizen would have computed his taxes in 1863. Joseph earned $9,000 in wages in 1862. His interest and dividend income came to $50. In 1862 Joseph also experienced a special situation covered by the new law. His father had died and left him an estate valued at $4,600. Joseph owed 1 percent of the estate's value as a legacy tax. Joseph figured his income tax first, adding his wages to his interest and dividend income ($9,000 + $50 = $9,050) and then multiplying the sum by 3 percent ($9,050 × .03 = $271.50). Then Joseph determined his legacy tax by figuring 1 percent of $4,600 ($4,600 × .01 = $46). Joseph calculated $271.50 + $46 to find his total tax of $317.50.

The new income tax did not raise as much money as expected to help pay for the war. Less than $3 million was collected in 1863, the first year that income taxes were due. Much of the difficulty in enforcing the tax law was caused by the tax collectors. They were poorly paid, and many quit before they completed their jobs. Some others were careless or corrupt. Although the income tax never raised as much money as planned, it did bring in more money each year, peaking at $73 million in 1866.

The federal income tax stayed in effect for 10 years and raised more than $340 million for the government during that time. The tax was repealed in 1872 and reinstated briefly in 1894. In 1913 the federal income tax that we have today was established.

Reading Time _____

Recalling Facts

1. The Civil War cost the U.S. government about
   - ❏ a. $3 million.
   - ❏ b. $3 billion.
   - ❏ c. $3 trillion.

2. The purpose of the Revenue Act of 1862 was to finance the Civil War through
   - ❏ a. raising duties on exports.
   - ❏ b. borrowing money.
   - ❏ c. taxation.

3. The Revenue Act of 1862 set the minimum taxable income at
   - ❏ a. $600.
   - ❏ b. $6,000.
   - ❏ c. $10,000.

4. The federal income tax raised
   - ❏ a. more revenue than expected.
   - ❏ b. about the revenue that was expected.
   - ❏ c. less revenue than expected.

5. The federal income tax established by the Revenue Act of 1862 stayed in effect until
   - ❏ a. 1866.
   - ❏ b. 1872.
   - ❏ c. 1913.

Understanding Ideas

6. One could infer from the passage that
   - ❏ a. incomes from $600 to $10,000 were among the lowest.
   - ❏ b. only upper-level wage earners were taxed.
   - ❏ c. most wage earners were taxed.

7. Based on the passage, one could conclude that
   - ❏ a. most people paid legacy taxes.
   - ❏ b. the income tax law stayed in effect for years after the war.
   - ❏ c. it was fairly difficult to figure out and file income taxes.

8. It is likely that the income tax law was repealed after 10 years because
   - ❏ a. the war had ended.
   - ❏ b. people disliked the law.
   - ❏ c. the government had paid off the war debt.

9. One could infer that the income tax brought in more money each year because
   - ❏ a. many more people were taxed at the 5 percent level.
   - ❏ b. more people were convinced it was for a good cause.
   - ❏ c. tax collection methods improved.

10. One could infer that the U.S. government preferred to tax people rather than borrow money because
    - ❏ a. it had to pay back the money it borrowed.
    - ❏ b. it could collect more money in taxes than it could borrow.
    - ❏ c. paying for the war with taxes had become accepted.

15 B   Civil War Revenue Stamps

In 1862 the U.S. government's debt from the Civil War was growing at the rate of $2 million a day. Besides introducing the federal income tax, the Revenue Act of 1862 also sought to raise money through the issue of revenue stamps. These were adhesive stamps that represented taxes on many legal documents and retail items.

There were 25 major types of taxed documents, including marriage licenses and property deeds. When a document was purchased, a revenue stamp was affixed for an additional charge. Most bank and personal checks and certain financial certificates were taxed according to the amount of the check or certificate. For example, amounts from $20 to $100 required a 5-cent stamp. Amounts from $100 to $200 required a 10-cent stamp.

Retail items that were considered luxury goods had revenue stamps already attached to them. The consumer paid the price of the item plus the tax. Among the taxed items were playing cards, gunpowder, feathers, telegrams, iron, leather, pianos, medicines, and whiskey. Medicines and perfumes required one 1-cent stamp for every 25 cents of the item's price. For example, playing cards cost 18 cents plus 1 cent for a tax stamp. The idea of a tax on goods was new to Americans in 1862. Consumers had to get used to being what today might be called "nickeled-and-dimed."

1. **Recognizing Words in Context**

   Find the word *affixed* in the passage. One definition below is closest to the meaning of that word. One definition has the opposite or nearly the opposite meaning. The remaining definition has a completely different meaning. Label the definitions C for *closest*, O for *opposite or nearly opposite*, and D for *different*.

   _____ a. started
   _____ b. removed
   _____ c. fastened

2. **Distinguishing Fact from Opinion**

   Two of the statements below present *facts*, which can be proved. The other statement is an *opinion*, which expresses someone's thoughts or beliefs. Label the statements F for *fact* and O for *opinion*.

   _____ a. Revenue stamp taxes should have been paid only by rich people.
   _____ b. Consumers paid the tax designated by the stamp plus the price of the item.
   _____ c. Marriage licenses were taxed.

3. **Keeping Events in Order**

   Number the statements below 1, 2, and 3 to show the order in which the events took place.

   _____ a. People paid taxes on retail items with revenue stamps.

   _____ b. Manufacturers attached revenue stamps to taxable retail items.

   _____ c. The Revenue Act of 1862 was passed.

4. **Making Correct Inferences**

   Two of the statements below are correct *inferences,* or reasonable guesses. They are based on information in the passage. The other statement is an incorrect, or faulty, inference. Label the statements C for *correct* inference and F for *faulty* inference.

   _____ a. The government had to find some way to raise money to pay off the war debt.

   _____ b. People disliked the tax on marriage licenses more than the tax on some other items, such as playing cards.

   _____ c. Revenue stamps were placed on items that the government hoped people would not use.

5. **Understanding Main Ideas**

   One of the statements below expresses the main idea of the passage. One statement is too general, or too broad. The other explains only part of the passage; it is too narrow. Label the statements M for *main idea,* B for *too broad,* and N for *too narrow.*

   _____ a. Revenue stamps were taxes on certain legal documents and consumer goods.

   _____ b. Revenue stamps were introduced by the U.S. government in 1862.

   _____ c. The government enacted a tax in order to raise money to pay for the Civil War.

Correct Answers, Part A _____

Correct Answers, Part B _____

Total Correct Answers _____

ANSWER KEY

READING RATE GRAPH

COMPREHENSION SCORE GRAPH

COMPREHENSION SKILLS PROFILE GRAPH

Answer Key

1A 1. b 2. c 3. a 4. a 5. b 6. a 7. c 8. b 9. c 10. b

1B 1. D, C, O 2. F, O, F 3. 2, 3, 1 4. F, C, C 5. B, M, N

2A 1. c 2. a 3. b 4. c 5. c 6. c 7. b 8. b 9. c 10. b

2B 1. D, C, O 2. F, O, F 3. 3, 2, 1 4. C, F, C 5. N, M, B

3A 1. a 2. c 3. c 4. b 5. b 6. b 7. a 8. a 9. a 10. c

3B 1. C, D, O 2. O, F, F 3. 2, 3, 1 4. F, C, C 5. M, N, B

4A 1. c 2. a 3. c 4. b 5. c 6. b 7. c 8. b 9. b 10. a

4B 1. D, C, O 2. O, F, F 3. 2, 3, 1 4. C, F, C 5. B, N, M

5A 1. a 2. a 3. b 4. c 5. b 6. c 7. a 8. c 9. c 10. a

5B 1. C, O, D 2. F, O, F 3. 3, 1, 2 4. F, C, C 5. B, M, N

6A 1. c 2. b 3. b 4. a 5. b 6. a 7. b 8. c 9. a 10. b

6B 1. D, O, C 2. O, F, F 3. 3, 2, 1 4. F, C, C 5. B, N, M

7A 1. c 2. a 3. b 4. b 5. a 6. c 7. b 8. c 9. b 10. a

7B 1. O, D, C 2. O, F, F 3. 2, 1, 3 4. C, C, F 5. M, N, B

8A 1. a 2. c 3. c 4. a 5. a 6. c 7. c 8. b 9. a 10. a

8B 1. C, O, D 2. O, F, F 3. 3, 1, 2 4. C, C, F 5. N, M, B

9A	1. b	2. b	3. c	4. b	5. c	6. c	7. a	8. a	9. c	10. a
9B	1. D, O, C	2. F, O, F	3. 1, 2, 3	4. C, F, C	5. B, N, M					
10A	1. c	2. a	3. b	4. b	5. a	6. b	7. c	8. a	9. c	10. a
10B	1. O, D, C	2. F, F, O	3. 2, 1, 3	4. C, F, C	5. B, M, N					
11A	1. c	2. a	3. a	4. c	5. a	6. c	7. a	8. a	9. b	10. b
11B	1. O, C, D	2. O, F, F	3. 3, 2, 1	4. C, C, F	5. M, N, B					
12A	1. b	2. b	3. c	4. b	5. a	6. b	7. c	8. c	9. c	10. a
12B	1. O, C, D	2. F, O, F	3. 1, 3, 2	4. C, F, C	5. B, M, N					
13A	1. b	2. c	3. b	4. c	5. a	6. b	7. c	8. c	9. a	10. b
13B	1. C, O, D	2. O, F, F	3. 2, 1, 3	4. C, C, F	5. B, N, M					
14A	1. b	2. c	3. a	4. b	5. c	6. b	7. b	8. a	9. c	10. a
14B	1. C, O, D	2. O, F, F	3. 2, 1, 3	4. C, C, F	5. N, M, B					
15A	1. b	2. c	3. a	4. c	5. b	6. c	7. b	8. b	9. c	10. a
15B	1. D, O, C	2. O, F, F	3. 3, 2, 1	4. C, C, F	5. M, N, B					

Reading Rate

Put an X on the line above each lesson number to show your reading time and words-per-minute rate for that lesson.

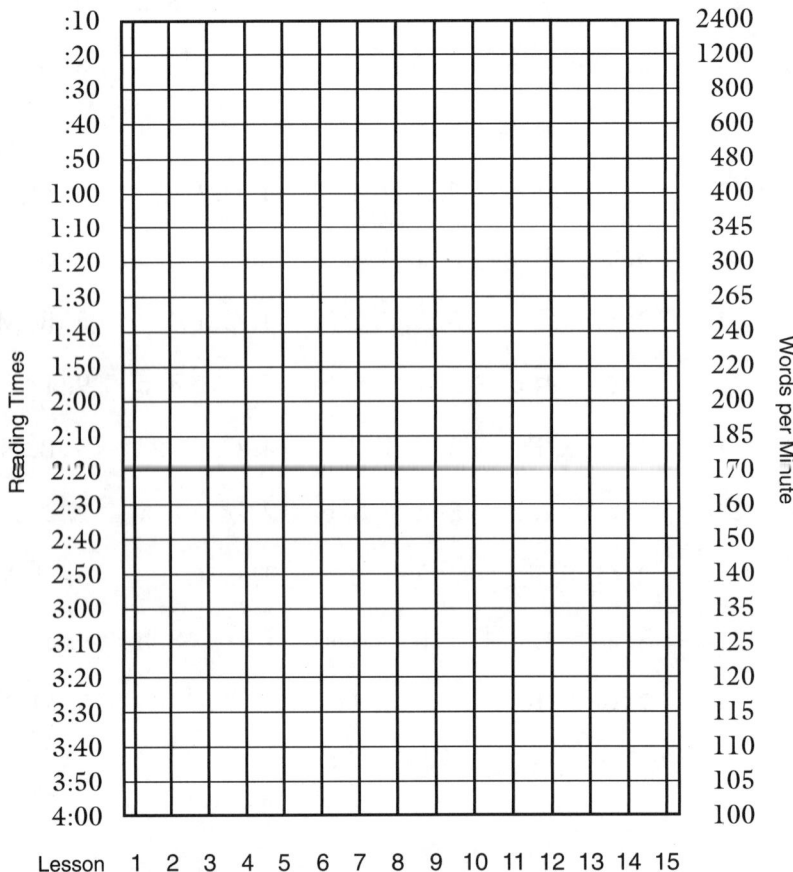

COMPREHENSION SCORE

Put an X on the line above each lesson number to indicate your total correct answers and comprehension score for that lesson.

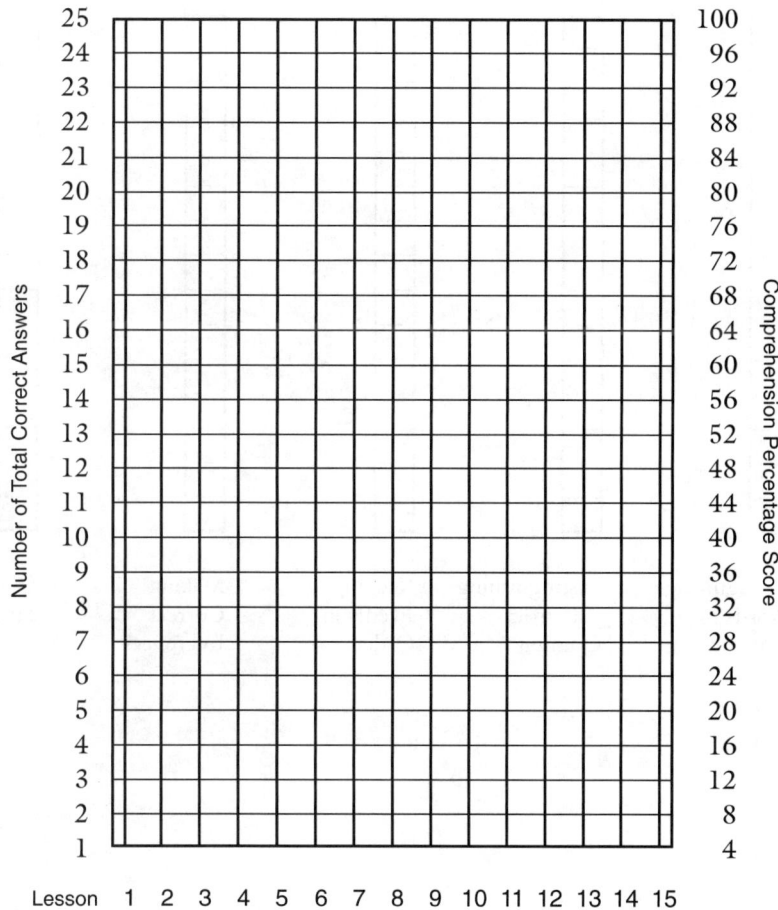

Comprehension Skills Profile

Put an X in the box above each question type to indicate an incorrect response to any part of that question.

Lesson 1
2
3
4
5
6
7
8
9
10
11
12
13
14
15

Recognizing Words in Context

Distinguishing Fact from Opinion

Keeping Events in Order

Making Correct Inferences

Understanding Main Ideas